The Oppositional Child

O. Randall Braman, Ph.D.

KIDSRIGHTS

Dedicated
to
Bessie Allain

THE OPPOSITIONAL CHILD

Copyright © 1997, 1982, O. Randall Braman, Ph.D.
Published by:
KIDSRIGHTS®
10100 Park Cedar Drive
Charlotte, NC 28210
800/892-5437 or 704/541-0100

10 9 8 7 6 5 4 3

Third Printing

ISBN: 1-55864-017-7

Table of Contents

Do You Know This Boy?   **1**

The Making of An Oppositional Child   **7**
Empathy: The Determining Factor   21
The Making of Pressuring Parents   25

Diagnosing Simple Uncomplicated Oppositionalism   **31**
Test Anxiety   33
Depression   34
Concealed Hostility   35
Feelings of Inferiority   37
Motor-Perceptual Difficulties   38
Low Risk-Taking   39
Alienation   41
Affectional Anxiety   42

Illustrative Cases   **47**
Mark W.   47
David E.   53
Scott K.   57
Chris F.   59
Steve D.   66
Eric B.   69

Chronic Underachievers   **77**
Illustrative Case - Kenneth T.   91

Patterns of Superficial Regression:
The Instrumentally Immature   **97**
    Illustrative Case - Shirley R.   113

Patterns of Superficial Regression:
The Pseudo-Mature   **119**
    Illustrative Case - Georgie C.   127

Patterns of Superficial Regression:
Transient Autistic Reactions   **131**
    Illustrative Case - Carl A.   138

The Habitually Hostile Child   **149**
    Illustrative Case - Terry G.   157

Oppositionalism in Children with Learning Disabilities **165**
    Distinguishing Oppositionalism From
    Learning Disabilities   167
    Pressuring the Learning Disabled Child   172
    Removing the Pressures   175
    Illustrative Case - Allen H.   176

High School and College Dropouts   **187**
    What's Wrong With C's?   195
    Illustrative Case - Roger L.   197

Unmaking Oppositionalism   **201**
    Rewarding Best Responses   203
    Letting Oppositional Behavior Exhaust Itself   207
    What If You Are Oppositional?   210

Suggested Readings   **215**

Introduction

Oppositionalism as a specific characteristic of personality was, apparently, described first in 1921 by Hermann Rorschach. "Tendency to opposition," as he called it (in German, oppositionstendenz), has remained a diagnostic factor in the Rorschach method of interpreting responses to ink blots, but has otherwise received little serious study by psychologists and psychiatrists.

My attention was originally directed to the concept of oppositionalism by Dr. G. Kinsey Stewart who, in 1956, took upon himself the task of teaching me Rorschach's psychodiagnostics technique. Later, in diagnostic and therapeutic work, and in vocational and educational counseling, I repeatedly found myself dealing with cases in which the problem seemed to me primarily or solely one which Rorschach would have most certainly called a "tendency to opposition."

As I began to feel that I understood the causal dynamics in these cases, I could see the same causal dynamics of oppositionalism at work in a wider and wider variety of cases.

Oppositionalism, as I now conceptualize it, is therefore

a much broader and more diverse personality characteristic than that originally described in 1921. But I would like to believe, and I feel that there is ample justification for this belief, that Hermann Rorschach, more than anyone else perhaps, would easily recognize what he was describing in 1921 in this broader and more diverse conceptualization.

This book is the product of clinical work with children under the Louisiana Department of Hospitals' Evaluation Center for Exceptional Children and the Louisiana Department of Health's Division of Maternal and Child Health, vocational and educational counseling of adults at the Tulane University Guidance Center, with Social Science Consultants in New Orleans, with the New Orleans Office of Vocational Rehabilitation, work at the University of Guam Counseling and Testing Center, and psychological research with the New Orleans Protestant Home for Babies.

Although all of these professional experiences have contributed significantly to the formulation of the specific ideas contained in this book, the most crucial has been the "Mental Health Clinic" held monthly and semi-monthly over an eight year period at the West Baton Rouge Parish Unit in Port Allen, Louisiana, under the Louisiana Department of Health.

Children referred to the "Mental Health Clinic" in Port Allen were given physical and psychological examinations, their parents and teachers were interviewed, and the findings discussed by the staff. As conclusions were reached, lengthy interpretive discussions were held with the parents, often involving several sessions.

Because of the small size of the community, and the relatively close mutual familiarity of its residents, it was possible, prior to their being seen at the clinic, and for weeks, months, and even years afterwards, to visit and chat informally with the parents and teachers of the children, and with the children themselves, in order to keep abreast of how things were going for the children and their families. Often, after a year or so, re-examinations were called for, and the children thus selected, their parents and teachers, were seen again with the entire process being repeated.

Because Port Allen's population was relatively stable during the years the clinic was in operation, and because of the staff continuity provided by the Director of the West Baton Rouge Health Unit, Dr. Marion J. Picinich, and the Unit's Public Health Nurses, Mrs. Bessie Allain and Mrs. Gladys Nelson, all three of whom were actively involved during its entire operation, and for many years afterwards doing follow-ups, the "Mental Health Clinic" at Port Allen provided unusual opportunities for discovering through long-range longitudinal studies the usefulness of psychodiagnostic categories and the effectiveness of different psychotherapeutic approaches.

It was in this context that "oppositionalism," in its diverse forms, began to be used by the staff as a diagnostic defining characteristic in more and more cases, with approximately twenty-three percent being labeled in final diagnosis as nothing more than some form of oppositionalism as described in this book. And it was in this context that the rather straightforward technique, as exemplified in this book, of simply explaining to parents how oppositionalism develops and how it can be avoided or eliminated was found to be the most effective approach for producing beneficial changes in their behavior, as well as their children's.

Acknowledgments

The "Mental Health Clinic" at Port Allen provided unusual opportunities for discovering through long-range longitudinal studies the usefulness of psychodiagnostic categories and the effectiveness of different psychotherapeutic approaches, because Port Allen's population was relatively stable during the years the clinic was in operation, and because of the staff continuity provided by the Director of the West Baton Rouge Health Unit, Dr. Marion J. Picinich, and the Unit's Public Health Nurses, Mrs. Bessie Allain and Mrs. Gladys Nelson, all three of whom were actively involved during its entire operation, and for many years afterwards doing follow-ups.

In addition to Dr. Picinich, who served as its congenial, tireless and everpatient director, and Mrs. Allain and Mrs. Nelson, who carried out the field work with diligence, tact and sensitivity, the Port Allen "Mental Health Clinic," during most of the years in which I was its psychologist, had the services of a remarkably capable Medical Social Worker, Miss Annie Louise "Polly" Thorpe.

Others who worked in the clinic or who contributed

significantly to its achievements are Dr. Ben Freedman, Dr. Marie Pareti, Dr. James Neely, Dr. James L. Harris, Dr. Carolynn Talley, Miss Ellie Magruder, Mrs. Mercedes Munson, Mrs. Leah Painter, Mrs. Kathleen Dodson, Mr. Patrick Chaudoir, Mrs. Violet Templet, Mrs. Dorothy Chance, Mrs. Deannie DeJean, and many others.

A conference on the Oppositional Child was held at the University of Guam. This conference was possible due to the support of President Antonio C. Yamashita, Mr. Alex C. Flores, Dr. Andrew W. Shook, Mr. Albert J. Rios, and Dr. Vincente R. L. G. Perez. Dr. Robert G. Wahler of the University of Tennessee, who has done research on the modification of oppositional behavior in children, was to be the featured speaker, but travel arrangements could not be worked out in time, and Dr. Russell G. Peckens of the University of Guam took his place.

In addition to Dr. Peckens and myself, Dr. Katherine B. Aguon and Mr. Jesus P. Cruz were panel speakers. The conference was by all indications successful. More than three hundred people attended, with a great deal of involvement in the discussions by the audience, and with the panel speakers being invited to speak at schools and other civic organizations on Guam repeatedly during the months following the conference.

Among those who helped to make the conference a success are Mr. Michael J. Vass, Mr. Wayne A. Hayden, Mrs. Karen E. Ford, Mr. Gregory Miles, Mr. Joseph C. Murphy, Mr. Paul J. Kahn, Mr. Joseph G. Chargualaf, Dr. Stanley Malkin, Mrs. Peggy Labbie Ayers, Mrs. Marie Flores Reyes, Mr. Juan Q. Fernandez, Mrs. Gloria Parrish Fernandez, Miss Sinfurosa Cruz, Mr. Pilika K. Palik, Mr.

Robert G. Kissell, and Mrs. Margaret Kimmey "Maggie" Reyes.

In addition to those mentioned above, there have been many people on Guam who, over the years, have taken special interest in the concept of oppositionalism. Their interest is in no small part responsible for the fact that this book was ultimately completed. Among the professors at the University of Guam, for example, Dr. Shirley K. Arriola introduced the topic of oppositionalism into her courses in personality and adolescent psychology, an academic recognition which strengthened my resolve to continue writing.

Later, during a long period when I had given up all hope of finishing the book, Dr. Solange Petit-Skinner, on her own initiative, submitted the beginning chapters of **The Oppositional Child** to several possible publishers, a concrete act of approbation galvanizing enough to once again set me to work at the task. Mr. Gary Wolverton, Mrs. Karen Huggins, Mrs. Lorna Liu, Mrs. Deborah Campbell, Mr. Del Northway, Miss Diane Gartland, and Mrs. Perlita Aquino are some of the people whose timely enthusiasm and insistence that the book was needed and of value made the writing easier.

The early chapters were read and skillfully edited by my former wife, Mrs. Devereux Braman; this in part accounts for the better quality of writing in the early chapters. My greatest appreciation, however, must be to Mrs. Edith Worsencroft, whose belief in the value of the book and in the fact that I would eventually complete it never wavered, and who even after she and her husband, Don, moved to Hawaii, continued to assist me in getting **The Oppositional Child** into print.

This book is dedicated, and rightly so, to Mrs. Bessie Allain, the indefatigable Public Health Nurse who persuaded everyone concerned that a psychological clinic for children was needed in Port Allen, Louisiana, and that I was the psychologist they should hire; her dedication was instrumental in holding together the fine staff we had there; she worked diligently herself and kept all of us working for eight productive years; she was deeply involved from the start as the concept of oppositionalism became understood and as the techniques for dealing with it evolved, and at the end, after I had come to Guam, she continued gathering follow-up information on children we had seen and sending it to me.

It is certainly no exaggeration to say that were it not for Mrs. Bessie Allain, this book could not have been written. Although usually not given to lavish praise, she once said of me that I had never made a mistake in diagnosis; although certainly not true, I use this remark of hers, everything considered, as my chief personal justification for having the temerity to present to others the ideas in this book.

There are those who I must name that made significant contributions directly and indirectly to the early development of my thinking concerning oppositionalism; these are Dr. Violet K. Richards, Dr. Albert W. Dent, Dr. Earl E. Larre, Dr. Lou LaBrant, Dr. Arvind Kumar M. Parikh, Mrs. Marion Andrus McCollam, Mr. Leonard S. Ungar, Miss Therese L. Faget, and Miss Sally Matlock.

There is no doubt at all in my mind that the conceptualization of oppositionalism as a situationally determined personality disturbance makes a much needed auxiliary to the standard psychodiagnostic system. In far too many cases, children are mislabeled for life as seriously mentally ill, or permanently learning disabled, or retarded, when their behavior is really only a normal, temporary, healthy, even intelligent and reasonable, self-conserving defense against pervasive parental pressure.

If all of this is true, and of course I think it is, then in closing I would like to acknowledge a debt to those teachers and professional colleagues who I feel helped to make me a better diagnostician: Dr. Charles F. Oberman, Dr. James R. Patrick, Dr. G. Kinsey Stewart, Dr. James L. Harris, Dr. Richard P. Vieth, Dr. William R. Sorum, Mr. John Charles Rosen, Mr. "Doub" Powell, and Mrs. Kathleen Dodson: and to the three people from whom I learned more about child psychology than from all the books I have ever read, namely my three children, Susan, Elizabeth, and Randall.

Finally, I want to thank my mother, Mrs. Lonnie Laub, who more than any other person inspired me to become a psychologist, and to my step-father, Paul S. Laub, who was instrumental in making this goal a reality.

O. Randall Braman
Tamuning, Guam

CHAPTER 1

Do You Know This Boy?

There is a boy that comes to my office almost every day and sometimes two or three times in a single day. He may be eight years old, or twelve, or sixteen. Sometimes he is stylishly dressed in the most expensive clothes, and sometimes he has on the cheapest of jeans or overalls. He may have red hair and be tall and lean, or he may be short and plump with dark hair and eyes. His mother or his father may bring him, or he may come alone.

He is a very pleasant person, usually quiet, friendly, and socially poised. Sometimes he acts as if seeing a psychologist and taking psychological tests are a burden, but usually he is interested in the situation. He has no difficulty in understanding directions or instructions, and may ask relevant questions about the psychologist and the test, being very careful not to offend.

Why has he come? What problem does he have that has caused him to need the services of a psychologist?

The story is always the same.

By the time he started school, it was already abundantly clear that he was bright. He was weaned and toilet trained a little earlier than the average, and except for some brief periods of bedwetting, constipation, or thumb-sucking, he was no real problem to his parents.

His coordination developed rapidly and he was alert to what went on around him.

After about the age of four, he had an occasional temper tantrum, was inclined to be stubborn at times and sometimes hard to manage. When his parents were in a hurry to go someplace, for example, he would usually dawdle at dressing, and it was easier for them to dress him than wait for him to do it.

On the other hand, when it was he that had someplace he wished to go he would frequently become greatly annoyed if they caused any delay. When it came time to go to bed, he could think of dozens of things that would put off this event, but when promised a gift or treat he insisted on having it immediately. He was always good at finding clever ways of getting around his mother, and would often say something she thought was funny enough to prevent her from becoming angry.

He usually did not hear when he was yelled at, and he was nearly as oblivious to his father as to his mother.

His father had ostensibly turned the child-rearing responsibilities over to the mother, and in the evening, when exasperated by something the boy did, would nag at the wife for not disciplining him better. The mother, although threatening the boy at times by telling him his father was going to punish him, welcomed the major parental role. She felt she knew exactly what kind of boy he was and what kind of man she wanted him to become. She only wished that her husband would take more time with him, or at least support her more in matters of discipline. She felt close to her son, and anyone observing the two together could see how similar they were in gesture and mannerism.

The father was ordinarily hard-pressed by his work and the demands of his social life. He frequently left the house on Saturday and Sunday mornings to fish or play golf with his friends and would come in too tired or busy for any casual activities alone with his son. The mother made it a point to have a baby-sitter often so she could join her husband in social activities.

Once or twice a year the family took a vacation together, and would travel four or five hundred miles a day seeing all the major sights. Frequently they joined other family groups for all day outings, and at such outings the grown-ups would play cards or talk together while all the children played around them. Cook-outs in the back yard were another popular activity, and the children played together while the grown-ups socialized.

The parents made whatever sacrifices were necessary to see that their son participated in all worthwhile activities, associated with the best children, and had his share of toys and equipment. Although he was eager to do or have whatever was available, he lost interest quickly. He found reasons for dropping out of activities and his toys were quickly broken or lost.

When he started to school his parents became active members of the PTA, and were strong supporters of academic improvements. They attempted to maintain close contact with the school, and were prone to be disparaging of parents who did otherwise. The mother missed no opportunity to meet and talk with her son's teacher in case he was having any problems in school, and in case there were anything she should know or do which would contribute to her son's full intellectual development. She was particularly interested in the I.Q. testing done at the school, and the teacher had confided to her that her son's I.Q. was high.

During the first and second grades the boy did fairly well in school. But in about the third or fourth grade he had a particularly difficult teacher. She was either too old, too inexperienced, or otherwise too unskilled or impatient to cope with the boy. She sent notes home warning that his school work was not satisfactory and that he tended to daydream and waste time in school. Typically, the unique contribution this teacher made was to be the first person who did not or could not evade the fact that there was a problem.

Previous teachers had been loath to face the parents with such a revelation. They may have used tricks on the boy to get him to do at least some of his work, but usually they just "rolled the sins forward " for a year, rationalizing that he was bright enough to be passed to the next grade even though he was essentially making no progress in his academic work.

The mother, who had always assumed the responsibility for seeing that her son did his homework, now sat down with him every night until it was completed. He frequently forgot what his assignment was, failed to bring home his books, or did not remember to take the completed work to school with him the next day. The sessions at home became longer, more emotional and more drawn out. The mother had to stay right by his side or he would do nothing.

The boy at such times seemed unable to understand the most simple explanations. For example, she drilled him relentlessly on spelling and he would repeatedly make the most ridiculous mistakes. If the father were there he would become angry at the child, and after trying himself unsuccessfully to get the boy to spell the words correctly would send him to bed in tears.

On some occasions he would spell the words correctly at home for his mother, and the next day at school misspell all of them on the test.

He finally failed a grade, was transferred to another school, and was seen by a school counselor, pediatrician, psychologist, and educational consultant. Depending on whom he saw and when he saw them, various diagnoses and remedies were offered. His vision was tested, his hearing examined, and basal metabolism measured.

When someone finally asked him what he thought was wrong, he answered that he guessed he was just lazy. But it seems now that he has always believed there is more wrong with him than this, and that he is shamefully lacking in some essential mental quality or ability that others around him apparently possess.

Although he has always seemed to get along well with other children, being something of a leader on the playground, his schoolwork remains poor. He might show interest and even talent in some activity divorced from his schoolwork, but the fact that he passes any courses in school can be credited totally to his mother's hard work and perseverance. If she ever relaxed for a moment, he would quickly be flunking in all his academic work.

This is the boy who waits in my office every day when I go there. This is the boy I've seen a thousand times. He waits in my office for me now, and in the office of every psychologist in the country. His name is legion. He is the **Oppositional Child**.

CHAPTER 2

The Making of An Oppositional Child

The child manifesting oppositionalism is not neurotic, at least not if one means by neurosis an internalized, self-sustaining maladjustment.

Although usually unaware of what he is doing, the Oppositional Child reacts specifically and adaptively to a pattern of parental pressures–pressures sometimes subtle but always so pervasive that usually there is really nothing constructive he can do but oppose them.

Oppositionalism may occur in emotionally disturbed children and adults, in the neurotic, psychotic, brain damaged and mentally retarded. But when oppositionalism is the only problem, psychiatric treatment is seldom required–a fact most convincingly obvious when one observes that in any area where the Oppositional Child is not being pressured his interests and competency are normal.

Were the parents to remove the pressures from those areas in which they maintain them, the child would quickly manifest normal interests and competency in these areas. Of course, the younger the child, the quicker changes occur.

Still, adults thirty and forty years of age, despite a lifetime of self-defeating oppositionalism, often change drastically for the better once completely out from under parental domination.

The parents of oppositional children may deny that they pressure their children. In fact, they are likely to be offended by such an accusation. They can give examples of how they do not insist that their children continue activities in which they have lost interest. Sometimes these parents are quite willing to let their children repeat a grade. They may even deny that they consider a college education necessary. And they are usually much too sophisticated to have any fixed ideas as to what their children should do as a career or life's work.

Where then is the pressure?

From the child's point of view the answer is clear. He is expected to excel, or at least come up to parental standards in all the activities which the parents feel are important.

If he fails in any respect, the parents see it as a personal failure which they must actively rectify themselves. They deprive the child of any opportunity to correct his own mistakes, to discover his own goals or to build stable levels of confident self-expectations. They expropriate his every achievement as their own, prevent him from experiencing the natural consequences of his actions and, under the guise of helping him avoid mistakes, force him to undertake tasks in the way they think is best.

Whenever he attempts something on his own they are careful to point out all the things he does wrong, for fear that he may be satisfied with inferior levels of achievement.

His hair could be combed better, his clothes could be neater, and his grades could always be higher.

There is a "but" at the end of every compliment. *"That's good, but you made the ears too big." "Well, I'm glad to see you are finally practicing, but that's not the right lesson." "I know you want to help, but I'm in a hurry."*

Since the child has no other source for his values, he first strives to meet his parents' ever receding standards. But with no solid rewards for his efforts, his confidence diminishes. He learns that it is hopeless to try. He is told repeatedly that if he would just apply some effort he could succeed, but whatever efforts he is able to muster are never enough to gain an unqualified gesture of parental approval. His parents use every achievement only as proof that he could do better.

The child sees himself as an extension of his parents' relentless strivings. They are counting on him, it seems, to establish them as parents and as people. His fears are their fears magnified, for he feels that his worth to them is dependent on what he is able to achieve. Affectional anxiety, namely the fear of loss of love, overwhelms him in the face of every task and test.

He must not let them down.

He must preserve the illusion for them that sooner or later he will bring home public accolades. Better not to try than to reveal mediocrity or ineptitude. Let others think you are lazy, but never, never reveal that which in your heart you fear most. For if parents should discover that you are not exceptional, that you are just a remarkably ordinary person, how could they love you? And your relatives and friends, how surprised and disappointed they would be to learn the truth!

Parents' anxieties about possible mistakes and errors are magnified a hundredfold in the Oppositional Child. He is a perfectionist who expects immediate success. He has learned all too well the lesson his parents taught: if you don't do something right the first time, there must be something wrong with you or with the way you do things.

Mistakes reflect inferiority; nice children from nice families don't make mistakes. Diligence and perseverance are virtues for the dullards. The "in" crowd and the gifted should succeed effortlessly and quickly. What does it profit a man if he gains the whole world, if he has to struggle for it and thus lose forever his illusions of superiority?

Oppositionalism appearing early in elementary school is nearly always due to maternal pressures. When it appears for the first time in high school or college the father is usually the one who is responsible. When only one parent is applying the pressure, the child blossoms the more he comes under the influence of the non-pressuring parent. When both parents are actively guilty, the child's oppositionalism remains chronic and appears intractable.

In large families the younger children are more likely to be buffered from parental pressures. Although the older children are frequently given unreasonable responsibilities with no authority for meeting them, and are blamed for any mistakes the younger children make, the younger children are given greater independence and freedom from parental control.

The rewards and punishments meted out by the older siblings, although often considered unfair or even harsh by adult standards, are straightforward and effective without the subtle undertones which make parental pressures so devastating. The younger children then tend to be more self-confident, irresponsible, and simply stubborn. They show less self-defeating oppositionalism, unless of course, as sometimes happens, the mother descends on her youngest child with the full force of all her frustrated yearnings. In this case, the youngest child will manifest the classic patterns of the Oppositional Child.

The pressures parents impose cannot be measured by how much they demand of their children. Many, if not most, pressuring parents demand little if anything of their children. The Oppositional Child is ordinarily quite bored with his existence.

Pressure is imposed in such cases by withholding commendations, by never indicating to the child that his past performance has been good. The parents grumble about his uncooperativeness, dwell at length on his faults, and make an issue of his every mistake. The pride they may take in their child and his achievements remains a secret. Every request or demand is backed up by a threat, and they can never believe that their child would do any of the things they wish him to do without such threats.

Oh, they may promise a new bicycle or other special treats if he achieves some cherished goal of theirs, but they are loath to offer the small spontaneous rewards that his ordinary efforts deserve. They fear that small gestures of unqualified parental approval will make him self-satisfied and will take away his motivation for further achievement. And the major prizes which they hold out for future achievement are seldom earned.

Once the parents discover that they child really wants the thing they promised, they use this knowledge as another means of threatening him, telling him that he will not get it if he does not do as they wish. Eventually, any enthusiasm the child may have had for the promised reward wanes, and he ceases to manifest any effort to attain it. Then the parent, angry yet unwilling to deprive the child, gives him whatever was promised and is bitter because the child seems so unappreciative.

Oppositionalism in children occurs in all socio-economic groups and in groups at all levels of educational attainment. The son of a college professor or bank president is no less likely to be oppositional than the son of a share-cropper or backwoods fisherman.

The degree of permissiveness of the parents shows no relationship to the frequency of oppositionalism in their children. Parents who are intimately involved with their children are as likely to produce oppositional children as parents who are aloof or rejecting. The amount and degree of punishment, physical and otherwise, used or not used by the parents has little bearing on how oppositional their children may be.

The single factor which identifies parents of oppositional children as distinct from parents of children who are not oppositional is their failure to recognize and reward the little, day-to-day, positive achievements of their children. Whatever the reason, parents who feel that their children's small victories are never worthy of honest recognition, who are too busy or too unsure of themselves to spontaneously praise their children's best efforts, will find that their children lose interest in achievement.

Parents who notice only their children's shortcomings, who find fault with whatever they do, and who consistently deprive their children of the joys that are to be had in their little daily successes, should not be surprised that their children give up trying. The constantly grumbling and complaining father and mother through their own efforts guarantee that they will have plenty to grumble and complain about.

Oppositionalism occurs when children feel that no matter what they do their actions will never be appreciated. Thus parents who make their children feel this way are the ones who have oppositional children.

Parents who never criticize but who are simply parsimonious in giving recognition pose a special problem. Such people are sometimes very pleasant and charming. They may give the impression that they are very supportive and desirable parents. But it is easy to see why their children have so many difficulties.

Simply withholding recognition from others is a very subtle form of hostility, one that leaves the hostile person innocent in his own eyes and in the eyes of others. No matter how loving and considerate they may otherwise be, parents who refrain from impulsively praising their children's achievements occasionally are very likely displacing some kind of hostility onto their children, and in so doing are undermining their children's confidence.

On the other hand, there are parents who have every fault imaginable, but who exclaim with obvious admiration whenever their children do anything that is a little better than they expected. Such parents may be impatient, aloof, and quick to lose their temper, but if they are empathic in recognizing little daily achievements, their children blossom. Such parents are seldom considered "ideal," and yet they give to their children self-confidence and the desire to achieve.

Such parents need not even be consistent in recognizing a child's little daily achievements; it is only necessary that they recognize some of them. When parents notice some particular action of their child which is deserving of praise and then give that praise quickly, emphatically and unequivocally, it does not matter that they may miss other things the child does which are equally deserving of praise.

The importance of rigid consistency in child-rearing practices is a Victorian myth which has no empirical evidence to support it. Children will forgive their parents almost any mistake or oversight, if at a given moment when they need it their parents come through. Inconsistency on the part of the parents only makes them seem more human in the eyes of the child and, if anything, causes the child to develop greater self-confidence and mature understanding.

This does not mean, however, that parents who are fundamentally preoccupied with their own well-being, who are more interested in their own problems and image than in the welfare of their children, can expect their children to respond positively to an occasional token of recognition. For recognitions to be effective they must be the product of real parental interest in and awareness of what the child is doing or attempting to do.

Far too many parents play the role of "the good parent" without regard to what the child does. Parents who lavish praise or love on a child, whether or not the child has done anything to prompt such displays of affection, are as destructive as parents who maintain a critical, punitive attitude. In either case the child is being ignored, and the worst thing one can do to a child, or to an adult for that matter, is to ignore him.

A child must feel that what he does matters. If the good things he does do not seem to matter to his parents, then he is forced to see whether what he does bad matters to them. By blind trial and error the child hunts for something that *does* matter to his parents, something that will shake their preconceptions and force them to recognize what their child is doing. All too often what the child eventually finds that breaks through their seeming indifference is doing exactly the opposite of what the parents would want him to do.

The Oppositional Child, as unaware as his parents are of what he is doing, is desperately attempting to become a full, participating member of the family. He vaguely feels that all his constructive behavior passes like a shadow in the eyes of his parents, who are lost in a preoccupation with their own problems and anxieties.

Within the interpersonal field of the family he must fill space, what he does must count for something. The more desperate he becomes, the more his mental energies are consumed in a frantic search for the vulnerable nerve of his parents. If the parents are so entrenched in their preconceptions or are so remote psychologically or physically that they are totally invulnerable, the child slips helplessly into chronic apathy and indifference.

But most parents are not so aloof and the reasonably bright child will eventually touch a nerve. When he does, the parent screams with anguish, thus assuring the child, for perhaps the first time, that in his parents' view what he does matters.

Probably one of the clearest indications that a parent is on a collision course with a child is a stated belief in some particular rule-of-thumb concerning child rearing. Parents who "believe in" this or that are in for a rude awakening. There is more than humor in the remark of the father who said that when he married he had three theories on how children should be raised, and now he has three children and no theories.

There are rules that parents should attempt to follow in being good parents, but these are not the kinds of rules most parents are looking for. A child is a complex bundle of individual traits with unique characteristics and potentialities. He is a dynamic, on-going, ever-changing organism with an endless repertoire of surprises.

The good parent is one who welcomes the child into the family without preconceptions, who helps him discover himself by applauding on the sidelines as the child tackles the tasks of growing up. The good parent offers help when the child wants it and needs it, but does not take over and do things which the child can and should do for himself. The good parent may worry when the child has problems and go in at night and look at him while he sleeps, but he never loses faith in his child's capacity to come through on his own. The good parent does not allow his child to sell himself short, but also does not harass and criticize his efforts.

Most of all, a good parent is always responsive to evidence that the child is constantly emerging into higher levels of maturity and responsibility.

It is by the little day-to-day recognitions that a child's character and personality are formed. The parent who pauses to give recognition only when his child does something a little worse than he ordinarily does is shaping the child's behavior away from what both he and the child want. The parent who remains blind to his child's real victories and achievements stifles his enthusiasm and confidence. The parent who has made immutable decisions about what he is going to believe his child is like, what his child can or cannot do, clamps a limit on his child's development.

The conversation of parents is often riddled with the blasphemies of despair. *"Mary is a poor eater," "Johnny hates to practice the piano," "I guess Freddie is just like me and will never be any good in arithmetic," "If I didn't stay after her she would never get her homework," "Oh, Lord, he's hard-headed!" "She's convinced we don't love her," "How do you get him to realize that he must study if he is ever to amount to anything?"* The number of ridiculous preconceptions that parents harbor about their children is amazing.

Without ever considering that they may be wrong, far too many pronounce one child bright or pretty and others dull, ugly, or lazy. A father may dote on his oldest daughter while being blind to the attributes of his other children. Not only is this destructive to the other children, it is usually so for the favored child as well. In the light of the vast untapped resources of talent, charm, beauty, and wisdom to be found in any child, it is inconceivable that a parent with even a modicum of sensitivity could for any period of time prefer one of his children over the rest.

Parents with rigid preconceptions concerning their children are like juries that condemn an accused man before the evidence is in. Children cannot be pre-judged if they are to develop confident self-identities. If parents do not help a child discover himself in terms of his own true strengths and weaknesses and do not let him make his own first feeble efforts and mistakes, they will find themselves alienated at every turn.

And oppositionalism is the only constructive defense a child has against parents who are dead set on making up to him for what they did not themselves have as children.

Opportunities thrust on a child before he gets the chance to develop the desire and confidence needed to take advantage of them can only cause him to resist. An energetic parent, girded to the loins with rigid beliefs about how a child should be treated and how he should react to such treatment, is well down the road to producing an Oppositional Child. The parent who never has the time to remark on something worthwhile his child is doing or attempting to do will find himself taking far more time later when the child breaks forth in open defiance. The parent who is too jealous of his own superior position to be willing to grant his child the pleasure of feeling competent himself will have plenty of time to ponder his own failings as a parent.

And there are worse things than oppositionalism. There is apathy and autistic withdrawal. There is the utter despair of a child crippled for life because his first attempts to gain love failed. There are children and adults for whom neither oppositionalism, apathy, autism, nor despair can remove them from the control of their domineering parents, and who become vacuous automata chirping the senseless preconceptions of their parents and living out their lives a lie to their own natural desires and potentialities.

In our society, where children are provided with opportunities for achievement undreamed of in other places and times, efforts must be made to prepare them psychologically for their challenges. Parents have the responsibility of sending their children to school eager and enthusiastic for learning. Both the parents and the teachers must preserve this eagerness and enthusiasm by emphatically recognizing the children's little day-to-day struggles and victories.

If we continue, as we all too often do now, to ignore or depreciate their efforts, criticize and chide them about their smallest mistakes, our children have no choice but to get us off their backs before they can be free to tackle the important tasks ahead of them. There are problems facing their world that we have not been able to solve, but which they are going to have to either solve or live with. They need to be going about the business of developing competency and wisdom to be men and women in that world. They need what help we can give.

But far too many of us are just burdening them with a negative approach to everything. Blind, desperate opposition toward us is in such circumstances the only rational thing they can do. If we are trying to teach them that only Mommy and Daddy know best, that without their parents' injunctions and directions they will be lost, then thank goodness a large portion of them are opposing us.

If we have burdened them with our own magnified anxieties and pumped them full of self-doubts and, instead of helping them to identify their own strengths, have criticized their every effort, then what else can they do but reject our teachings? The world has always had oppositional children, and perhaps this is not altogether bad. If we have more now than ever before, it may be because parents now need opposing more than ever before.

Oppositionalism, as bad as it is, is a constructive response to parental pressures. There is no doubt that it, more than any other thing children can do, causes parents individually and collectively to stop pressuring them. Once his parents finally give up, a child may be able to learn to take charge of his own life. If he is lucky, the only thing he loses is fifteen to twenty years of his life.

But, unfortunately, oppositional children all too often have the habit of becoming in their turn pressuring parents, ready to repeat the whole process the next generation.

Perhaps it is time that we took stock of ourselves, as parents and as people, and tried to understand and prevent the senseless tragedy of oppositionalism in our children.

Empathy: The Determining Factor

The most significant aspect of the relationship between the Oppositional Child and his parents is the empathy they feel for each other. If it were not for this close emotional involvement, the pressures maintained by the parents would not have such devastating effects on the child. And the parents, on the other hand, would not be so dedicated to this pressuring if they did not feel such a close identity with the child.

Empathy is the capacity to feel what others feel. It is the psychological quality which more than anything else is characteristically human. It is the greatest achievement of mankind, yet it makes people more vulnerable to the weaknesses, cruelties and thoughtlessness of others. It prevents a person from enjoying cruelty, but forces him to be cruel when the welfare of others is at stake. It serves as the only real basis for love yet turns brother against brother and son against father. It transforms transient shame into life-long guilt and permeates the individual with unresolvable conflicts. It drives people into despair and madness, yet is their main strength for maintaining or recovering rationality.

The capacity for empathy is man's burden and his glory, and it is the greatest gift parents can give to a child.

But, once given, empathy is a terrible taskmaster. The empathic child cares, and because he cares so much he is without defense. Treating such a child as if he is insensitive or unfeeling compels him to construct defenses against such treatment. By these defenses he attempts to convey to his parents, to the world, and to himself, that he in fact does not care. But behind these defenses he suffers the agony of knowing that he has failed his parents and himself, and thus has failed as a human being.

How easy it would be, one thinks, to break this pattern, to take time off from the pressuring disparagement, and remark on something the child has done that has made the parent happy and proud. How easy it would be, yet how difficult to get some parents to do it.

The parents of oppositional children see themselves locked in a contest of wills with their children. They sometimes see their task as one of breaking their children's stubborn perversity like one would break the wildness of a mustang by riding it to exhaustion. But even horse-trainers have learned that this method has extremely undesirable consequences and should never be used with an animal of value. How even more unlikely that it would work with those most complex of all organisms, more valued than anything in this world, our children.

One should not confuse oppositionalism with ordinary stubbornness. A stubborn child may also be oppositional which makes a particularly formidable defense. But how stubborn a child is has nothing to do with whether or not he will be oppositional. Stubbornness, that is, the quality of being difficult to persuade when one's mind is made up, or negativism, which is not wanting to do whatever is suggested or required, are obviously learned forms of behavior that may appear similar to oppositionalism. But oppositional children are frequently neither stubborn or negativistic, and there are many stubborn and negativistic children who are not at all oppositional. The stubborn or negativistic child sulks, pouts, and refuses to do what you wish him to. The Oppositional Child, while frequently appearing to be cooperative, ends up doing exactly the opposite of what you want him to do and, which is even more important, he ends up also doing the opposite of what he himself wants to do.

Stubborn negativistic children are simply manifesting forms of behavior which they have found gratifying and pleasurable. These traits can easily change into persistence and determination once the individuals become involved in challenging and interesting tasks or careers.

Oppositionalism, on the other hand, is self-destructive. It occurs in sensitive, empathic children who believe themselves to be the bane of their parents' existence, an idea conveyed to them by their parents. Seldom do parents really intend to convey such a drastic notion to their children, but words and actions which would have no significant effect on non-empathic children may seriously damage the self-image of empathic children.

Thus the psychological quality within oppositional children which makes parental pressure and criticism intolerable is their empathy. They acutely feel the annoyance and disappointment they are causing their parents. Despite whatever they may do, they continually find themselves in the well-worn ruts of parent-child conflict, and for them there is no way out.

To whom can a person turn if he has failed to please the most important people in his life? Where can he hide if he fails to measure up in the eyes of his parents, whose values are the only ones he knows?

Thus the Oppositional Child must reject his parents and their values. In order to salvage his identity and meaning as a person, he must with all his mind and energy annihilate their significance in his life. If he is ever to be free, he must destroy the image of himself they have imposed on him. He must oppose their values, the way they dress, and the way they talk.

And, in all this, it matters not at all in what ways his parents may be right or wrong, innocent and guilty, wise or foolish. All must be thoroughly rooted out because, and this seems almost paradoxical, he knows them so well that he is always immediately aware of what they would think or feel about each thing he does. To him it always seems that Mommy and Daddy are watching over his shoulder at all he is doing–criticizing, pointing out his mistakes, and blaming him for his shortcomings.

Yet this capacity to empathize with his parents, which is at the root of all his problems, accounts for why the Oppositional Child is not as emotionally disturbed as he feels or appears to be. The intensity of his reaction to his parents reveals his potential for forming new emotional relationships once the psychological struggle with his parents is set aside.

If oppositionalism is his only problem it is because his parents, despite all their failings, nurtured and reinforced his capacity to empathize. They may have thoughtlessly abused this quality in their child later, but they must be credited with having implanted it in the first place, for empathy does not develop if it is always abused. And, once out from under parental domination, the Oppositional Child's chances of overcoming his self-destructiveness are totally dependent on how well developed is his capacity for empathy.

The Making of Pressuring Parents

Although it is a fact that oppositional children tend to grow up to become pressuring parents, the dynamics are undoubtedly more complicated than this. In order to understand what has happened that causes parents to pressure children, one must realize that parents not only train children but that children train parents as well.

Empathy between the mother and the child develops in a reciprocal manner. It would not be too fallacious to describe the infant as an automated teaching device who rewards its mother with smiles and coos when she does the right thing and who, by screaming at the top of its lungs, punishes her unmercifully when she does the wrong thing.

The effectiveness of this primitive training procedure can be observed in how quickly the young, inexperienced mother (and father!) become proficient in anticipating the needs of the infant. And, long before any deliberate attempts are made on the part of the parents to train the infant, it in turn learns by means of subtle rewards and punishments to discriminate between the activities and moods of its parents.

The infant becomes particularly conditioned to warning signs which indicate that its mother is not at the moment prepared to meet the infant's needs should they arise.

Through the pain and deprivation it experiences when its mother's attention is elsewhere, the infant learns to react anxiously when its mother is preoccupied, nervous, irritable, or impatient. By the rewards it receives when its mother is pleasant and attentive, the infant learns to be calm and relaxed when its mother is calm and relaxed. Thus with the mother and infant making each other relaxed or anxious as they themselves are relaxed or anxious, there begins the nucleus of empathy between them. In other words, they begin to feel what each other feels, sharing in a primeval way each other's emotions.

As a result of these frequent interchanges of rewards and punishments the mother begins to feel that she "knows" the child, understands its needs and even can read its thoughts. She feels at one with the child and is proud of her exclusive position in this respect. In most cases, it is this closeness to her child which makes the mother feel she is really a mother. The child at the same time blossoms in this relationship, and its obvious well-being and responsivity serve as powerful reinforcements for how the mother feels.

Now all of this intimate psychological involvement of the mother and child is necessary and good if the child is to develop into a normally responsive and empathic adult. But in this involvement also lies the germ of later parent-child conflict.

The mother realizes, of course, that she has a life separate from her child, and she never forgets this no matter how obsessive she may be with the role of motherhood. But to the mother, the child does not have, nor seem to need, a life separate from hers. She feeds him, bathes him, clothes him, and anticipates his every whim or problem. She drifts comfortably into the belief that "Mama knows best," and the actions of the child clearly confirm this. All the anxieties and self-doubts she may have had during the child's early post-natal development are now laughingly discounted. She has been tested and tempered by experience and has proven herself worthy. She is now an American Mother and is sure of herself, and sure of her understanding of her child.

Once she has been launched on this obvious collision course with her child, the usual mitigating factor is her husband. Many husbands fortunately rise to the occasion and, without being aware of what they are doing, tend to curb their wives' maternal zeal. They ordinarily do this by responding to their children's individuality. Being away from the home more, and being blissfully unaware of their wives' subtle stratagems, they blunder in and disrupt the mother-child coalescence.

When this happens, most wives accept it philosophically and, with only minor pangs or regret, abandon their attempts to be their children's sole mentors. Before they have time to realize what is happening, they see their children emerging as individuals quite different from what they had planned.

For those mothers who can accept it, who find themselves pleased and proud of their children's newly developing independence, there begins for them a much richer and ultimately more rewarding relationship with their children.

But many mothers do not give up so easily. What they cannot salvage by subterfuge they take by force, and their husbands either approve of this or acquiesce for lack of confidence. The husbands then find themselves and their views excluded, and may rationalize that it is not their job to rear the children. Wives thus left with a free hand, without the balancing perspective which only their husbands could provide, begin the fatal process of attempting to mold their children to fit idealistic preconceptions.

Unfortunately for all concerned, children frequently respond to this sort of treatment at first by living up to their mothers' fondest expectations. When, from time to time, they fall a little short of the routine perfection expected of them, their mothers quickly learn that a little stern pressure will set them straight. And when, by about the third grade, these little necessary pressures have grown to an almost continuous pattern of harassment and criticism, the husbands are forced to re-enter the scene.

One would think that the husbands would now clearly see the need to rectify their earlier errors of omission and attempt to get their wives to let their children out from under the constant pressure. But strange as it may seem, the husbands at this point usually reveal that all along they have been endorsing their wives' child-rearing practices, and with their wives' insistence and encouragement they begin to supplement the feminine pressure the children had been receiving with the more fierce masculine type. When this stage is reached, the parents find themselves united in a common cause confronted by children who oppose them every step of the way.

Of course in many cases parents fall into the habit of pressuring their children for less complicated reasons. Often they see eye-to-eye from the first on how children should be reared, and discover together how easily children can be controlled by forcing them into line. When their children seem particularly resistive, they simply do what has worked so well in the past, that is, increase the pressure. Along the line they learn that "reasoning" with their children works only if they can create a little fear or guilt in them, and that by pointing out to their children how selfish, inadequate, or helpless they are their children become more pliable.

No matter how it may develop in particular cases, parents learn to pressure their children for the same reason children learn to oppose their parents. On each side those techniques are learned which work, which get them through crises, which postpone uproars, or which allow the participants to make it through the responsibilities of another day.

To an observer, the meager pleasure that parents obtain from the grudging obedience of pressured children may hardly seem worth the effort. But it must be remembered that parents of oppositional children, as far as their role as parents is concerned, become just as discouraged and desperate as their children. And, like their children, they continue to do what they have done in the past because under the circumstances there is little else they can do.

CHAPTER 3

Diagnosing Simple Uncomplicated Oppositionalism

Simple, uncomplicated oppositionalism seldom occurs in a child who is not at least average or above average in intelligence. The parents of such a child are typically well-meaning and intelligent themselves. They do not bring the full force of parental pressures on their child unless there has been some objective evidence that he is bright.

They want the best for him, and take seriously their responsibilities in this respect. They love their child, and care what happens to him. They take pride in their parental roles, and feel involved with their child. They wish him to avoid the mistakes they made. They want him to be better educated and more socially skilled. They want him to have status and social acceptance. They are distraught when he does not progress satisfactorily in school, and they are saddened when they begin to realize how unhappy he is.

As many as one in every ten children seen in a psychological clinic may suffer from nothing more than simple uncomplicated oppositionalism. When the parents of such children are told in a straight-forward fashion what they are doing and are made to realize its full effects, at least some of them drastically reduce the degree of pressure immediately. Parents may come to the clinic literally at their wits end, yet when they learn the cause of their problem are frequently surprised how very simple it is. Of course, such parents are unable to change their basic attitudes and the aspirations they have for their children, but they can change enough of their essential behavior toward their children to eliminate oppositionalism.

Giving the child the opportunity to live his own life is not easy for parents that care so much. But because they care they can try. And, as strange as it may seem, all the child needs is for them to try. The younger the child is, the quicker he forgives his parents all their mistakes.

The parent of the Oppositional Child has erred only in doing too much. He has succeeded far more than he realizes in establishing his own values, anxieties, and aspirations in the child. He must relax his hold on the child much sooner than he feels it is safe to do so. He must have faith in his child, and faith in his own teachings and example. He must let the child tackle his own world on his own. This takes courage and love, but it does not take more courage or more love than most parents have for their children.

Since some parents are able to rectify the problem as soon as it is explained to them, it is imperative that the professional person, the psychologist, pediatrician, psychiatrist, social worker, school counselor, teacher and school administrator, physician and nurse, are able to recognize accurately the clinical signs of simple, uncomplicated oppositionalism and explain its dynamics to parents.

Parents themselves can avoid many of the problems of oppositionalism by learning to identify its causes, characteristics, and consequences.

Test Anxiety

The Oppositional Child is typically described as being indifferent to his school work, lazy, and unmotivated. Among the first things the psychologist can observe in the Oppositional Child is how untrue is this description.

The simple, uncomplicated Oppositional Child reflects anxieties immediately and he centers on how difficult the test is, how well he is doing, and whether he "passed" or not. He is sometimes extremely reluctant to say he does not know the answer to a particular question, and in such cases it is like "pulling teeth" to get him to admit this. He usually understands the directions immediately but frequently misses some of the first easy items of each subtest. As a particular task gets underway, his concentration improves and he becomes absorbed in his work. But if he runs into a difficulty, his performance will deteriorate in predictable ways and he will rigidly repeat incorrect responses. Anxiety may constrict his visual field, making him miss obvious essential details.

His oppositional characteristics are manifested most clearly in motor-perceptual difficulties and reversals. A fine tremor may develop in his hands and they may begin sweating as the tension mounts. He is annoyed by the ticking of the stop watch, and repeatedly verbalizes self-disparaging statements.

With each new task, he exclaims how easy it is, but his mind wanders and he cannot concentrate or remember what he is supposed to know or do. When he makes a mistake, he is harsh in his self-criticism. Present him a page of arithmetic problems or words to read, and he immediately locates the ones he cannot do, and is indignant that they are there. When he finally is finished and leaves, the exhausted psychologist leans back in his chair and wonders how anyone could describe this child as indifferent, lazy or unmotivated.

Depression

All oppositional children are unhappy. In many cases the child's unhappiness is manifested obviously in his behavior and expression. He is bitter, discouraged, resentful, and pessimistic. He views any efforts to help him as a waste of time.

To himself, he is a hopeless case.

Anxieties about the tests and psychological evaluation may tend to conceal the pervasive depression present, but the alert psychologist will find ample signs. In his drawings there may be large portions of his picture darkly shaded. When anxiety and impulsivity are under control, or when he is not preoccupied with racing the stop-watch, his reaction times are slow. He responds especially slowly to those ink blots of the Rorschach which contain large dark areas, and he usually reports seeing dark ominous objects in them. With older oppositional children and adults, objective personality tests always reveal high depression scores.

Concealed Hostility

The Oppositional Child is, of course, absolutely frustrated. In resisting parental pressures, he thwarts himself. In opposing his parents' desires and aspirations he opposes his own, for he has absorbed completely their interests and values.

Hostility is the natural reaction to frustration, but he can seldom vent these hostilities directly. Being the recipient of the unsparing love of his parents and of every material and psychological advantage that his parents can provide creates in him a feeling of worthlessness.

He is well aware of how he has failed his parents, and his guilt would become intolerable if he allowed a direct expression of hostility to occur towards his parents. An enormous amount of mental energies, therefore, are consumed in attempting to control the underlying hostility. The more successful he is in this, the more pervasive is his depression and hopelessness.

If impulsive outbursts of hostility do occur, he becomes locked in a circular bout with anxiety, his impulsivity increasing his anxiety, and anxiety making self-control even more difficult.

Extreme cautiousness on such psychological tests as the Porteus Mazes, hesitancy in writing with many false starts and frequent erasures, and elaborate procrastination before undertaking a task reveal the habitual safeguards he maintains against his own hostile impulsivity. Usually these mechanisms are only temporarily effective, and his pencil pressure becomes so great that he may break the lead. He may accidentally knock over the object on which he is working or in some other way break the tension by destroying the effectiveness of his efforts.

He frequently manifests an endless number of subtle but seemingly calculated devices for frustrating the psychologist; he hands back objects he was supposed to hold and places those he was supposed to hand back out of the psychologist's reach.

On the Wechsler Block Designs he insists on matching up the sides when he is told explicitly that only the tops are to be duplicated, or he ponders over a question or task long after it is obvious that he has given up.

The "blood and guts" responses he sometimes makes to the Rorschach ink blots reveal his anxiety and hostility. Although the typical Oppositional Child shows ample signs of empathy, affection, and sensitivity on the Rorschach, the female elements are seen as "crabs", "storm clouds", or "decapitated witches", while the masculine elements are equally threatening. It is clear that emotionally he is geared for "flight or fight", but he is caught in a psychological trap from which he cannot begin to escape.

Feelings of Inferiority

Although the Oppositional Child will cling tenaciously to his self-image as a superior person, he always suffers secretly from an overwhelming sense of inferiority. Some children when asked to draw a picture of a person will draw a child of their own sex and approximate age with a flat head, the significance of which is obvious. And it is equally obvious what it means if this flat head is hidden under a hat of darkly shaded-in hair.

The child who draws the human figure with a square body conveys that he feels pressured to achieve more socially and academically than he feels he comfortably can. And if he sketches in the outer boundaries of the body with light shading it means that affectional anxiety, the fear of loss of love, is an integral part of all his relations with his parents and others around him.

Feelings of inferiority are, of course, the major source of his test anxiety, and he will nearly always reveal this in his remarks and actions during testing. In the older child or adult, the pattern of his answers on objective personality tests always shows how prone he is to exaggerate his weaknesses and minimize his strengths despite a strong need to prove his inherent superiority.

Motor-Perceptual Difficulties

Clinically, the most convincing evidence of oppositionalism in a child is the striking pattern of reversals which repeatedly occur in most motor-perceptual tasks. Teachers and parents invariably discover these difficulties in the child. He reads the word *"saw"* as *"was"*, makes his S's and N's backward, and in spelling reverses the last two letters of words like *"over"* and *"health"* which become *"ovre"* and *"healht."* What one is not so prone to have noticed is how often on arithmetic tests he subtracts when he is supposed to add, and how often he reverses the sequence of numbers read to him orally.

In administering tests, the psychologist observes all this and more. On the Wechsler Block Designs, for example, figure-ground reversals are obtained, and sometimes designs are completed perfectly upside down or as mirror-images.

His memory span for numbers is sometimes higher when the instructions are to give them in reverse (digits backward) than when he is to recite them as they are given (digits forward).

On the Rorschach, he develops his concepts whenever he can from the white spaces using the ink blot itself as background. When using symbols or codes, as on the Wechsler, he may lose considerable time in having to erase those he draws upside down or in reverse. He sometimes does his Bender designs in part or in whole upside down, and if not watched carefully will turn the cards to correct his mistake or make the task easier.

Even more confusing to the psychologist, on the Bender

he sometimes has difficulties with corners, drawing a line in the opposite direction from what he intended and then bringing the line around in the correct direction leaving at each corner something which appears to be the kind of "ear" which is indicative of brain dysfunction.

Since children suffering from minimal brain dysfunction are typically pressured by their parents, and thus are very likely to show all the manifestations of oppositionalism in addition to the organically determined disturbances of perception, it is at best no easy task to rule out some sort of brain dysfunction in the etiology of ordinary oppositionalism.

In the light of the seemingly incomprehensible and intractable difficulties they seem to have with motor-perceptual tasks, it is no wonder that theories of brain dysfunction, faulty cerebral dominances, and dyslexia have been accepted by both clinicians and parents alike as explanations of oppositionalism in children.

Low Risk-Taking

Oppositional children are afraid to try. What they would most like to do is what they most carefully avoid. They would much rather consider themselves "lazy", and have others do so, than risk their self-image in an honest attempt to achieve some cherished dream or goal. To them it is better to have never loved at all, than to have loved and lost.

It is their fear of loss of love that undermines their confidence. Their efforts have been so frequently criticized or ignored that they routinely expect failure. They feel that their parents will not forgive failure, that the only way they can maintain their parents' love is to maintain the illusion of their intrinsic superiority.

They yearn for quick, easy successes that do not require a public commitment. They dream of bringing home trophies of easy successes so they may bask in their parents' adulation.

But they ridicule the steady plodder, as they fear they would be ridiculed if they diligently pursued modest goals.

They entrench themselves in the role of the brilliant, promising youth who is charming but lazy. And they carry on an elaborate pattern of evasions and rationalizations in order to maintain this role. And their parents, to no small degree, support them in this undertaking, for they would rather have illusions of success than risk real failures.

Since the Oppositional Child's values and anxieties are those of his parents, only magnified, he is most likely to avoid those tasks or goals which are most important in his parents' eyes. For these are the ones which are most important to him. To commit himself to these tasks or goals and fail, or achieve only modest success, would be shameful and would most likely bring on a concerted barrage of criticism from his parents.

The English teacher's son, therefore, cannot read. The professor's son drops out of college. The minister's son becomes a "black sheep". And the physician's son hates medicine.

Alienation

Oppositional behavior creates a gulf between the child and his parents, forcing the child to find some area where he can risk applying himself. It is better in such cases if the parents are narrow and attempt to restrict the child to a limited number of activities. The child is still left with vast areas of worthwhile pursuits which he can possess as his own.

Domineering fathers who have insisted that their sons are going to be doctors have been instrumental in producing many of our best lawyers, artists, and novelists.

Some of our greatest women statesmen and scientists have come from homes where it was an inviolable rule that women are to be wives and mothers only, nothing else.

When the parents' demands are narrow and restrictive, the pressured child, although often burdened with lingering loneliness and guilt, can frequently find success outside these parental limits.

But the modern emancipated and liberal parents are not narrow or restrictive. *"Whatever my son wants,"* they say, *"is all right with us, just so long as he is successful."* Combine this seemingly enlightened view with the kind of parental pressures which produce oppositionalism, and the only alternative the child has is to fail. And he generally must fail in everything, for, no matter what he may show some casual interest in, his parents are quick to appropriate it as their own.

How often one sees a mother who professes to be showing her child how to do something and only succeeds in demonstrating how much better she can do it than the child can. How quickly such a mother gets impatient if the child does not respond as she expects him to. And fathers are perhaps even quicker to lose patience when their sons or daughters seem unable or unwilling to come up to their expectations.

The children of pressuring, preoccupied, or critical parents are drawn like magnets to those persons or groups where they and their actions are acceptable.

So while the parents continue on, grumbling or blissfully oblivious to what is happening, their children move out from under their influence. And unfortunately this is more than a "generation gap," for children thus alienated do not form new emotional involvements easily. In their desperation they may strive for feelings of belongingness within their peer groups, they may frantically try to outdo each other in order to establish their loyalty and position within these groups. But basically they suffer from a penetrating loneliness, a loneliness that could only be removed by unequivocal proof that their parents accept them for what they are.

Affectional Anxiety

The Oppositional Child not only feels he is not loved; he feels he is not lovable. He would usually deny this vehemently even if it were his habit to punish his parents by accusing them of not loving him. He strives to maintain the illusion that he is loved in the same way that he attempts to maintain the illusion that he is brilliant. Just as his laziness serves as a rationalization for why his brilliance never becomes manifest, his oppositional behavior serves as a rationalization for why his parents cannot demonstrate their love. But he is just as afraid to make an honest bid for parental love as he is to work diligently for academic goals.

Clinically, affectional anxiety is revealed when the child is asked to draw a picture of a person or when he is administered the Rorschach ink blots. The person who yearns for love but feels he is unlovable frequently draws the human figure with shaded, sketchy lines and on the ink blots sees fleecy clouds or fog.

The girl or young woman who draws the female figure with shaded, sketchy lines or who sees the female elements in the Rorschach as clouds or fog is unsure of herself as a woman, feels her femininity is not lovable, does not feel comfortably feminine, and has not made a confident feminine identification.

She may have learned to compensate for these feelings by acting exaggeratedly feminine, either by being extremely passive in a feminine manner or by being aggressively sexual. She may have learned to play the feminine social role with ease and proficiency, but her basic femininity remains stunted because her parents, particularly her father, did not respond to her little-girl gestures of love. In such young women sexual promiscuity may occur as typical oppositionalism or as a manifestation of the need to be loved as a woman, or both.

Affectional anxiety is just as devastating to the male as

it is to the female. Constant parental criticism of boyish traits and actions threatens the confidence of youths and forces them to search for proof of their manhood in areas often not approved by the family or society. It is not surprising (when you can get them to do it) that young toughs so often draw the male figure with shaded, sketchy lines and see the male elements in the ink blots as clouds or fog.

In young men, young women, children and adults the only effective therapy for affectional anxiety is finding sources of unqualified acceptance. The Oppositional Child has learned that it is futile to turn to his parents for this kind of acceptance, and therefore he tries to reject them and their values. But he is caught in a web of internal conflicts, for no matter how skillfully he may hide it, basically he respects his parents and shares their values.

Unaware of what is going on inside oppositional children, parents continue their grumbling and complaining never realizing that they, and they alone, have the remedy. And the child, equally unaware, seeks in those activities and places disapproved of by his parents for that which his parents seem unable or unwilling to provide, namely, unequivocal recognition for himself as a valuable person, respected, admired and accepted. It is as if he says, *"If I am no good, then let me find someone who will admire me because I am no good."* And sure enough, he can usually find someone who will give this kind of acceptance.

In the case of the Oppositional Child, his parents have done too good a job of indoctrinating him into their attitudes and beliefs. When they fail to sit back and enjoy the fruit of their efforts, when they continue to reproach and depreciate what they should be applauding and extolling, the child cannot simply ignore them.

In despair he opposes them, in desperation he seeks others who will accept him, but he never loses his affectional anxiety until he feels lovable in the eyes of Mommy and Daddy. And it is an unfortunate fact, especially disastrous for the Oppositional Child, that Mommy and Daddy are typically the last of all to pay their respects. When they do, if they ever do, the child may have become an adult who no longer needs or values their recognition, or who has become so hopelessly crippled emotionally that parental recognition for him comes too late and is far too little.

CHAPTER 4

Illustrative Cases

The following cases, and others appearing in this book, are
taken verbatim from the author's diagnostic reports and
from diagnostic reports of other psychologists prepared for
psychiatrists and mental health agencies. Identifying data
have been eliminated. No attempt has been made, however,
to change the findings in order to make them conform better
to the discussions concerning the characteristics of
oppositional children.

    The reader will notice that in these reports by
psychologists, in the interview materials, and in the
comments and conclusions of the social workers, public
health nurses, teachers and parents, a variety of terms and
phrases are used to describe oppositional traits and
behavior. This, however, should not prevent one from
discerning the oppositional characteristics present in each
child.

Mark W.

    Mark is six and one-half years old, and is being seen in
the clinic in August just before he enters the second grade.

Both of his parents are college educated. A psychological evaluation was requested because he was somewhat of a behavior problem in the first grade, and his parents want to know if he is too advanced for the class he is in. His mother feels that perhaps he became a behavior problem because he was bored. She says that when he is home she cannot think of enough things to challenge him with to keep him busy.

His teacher agrees that from the first few weeks of the first grade he could read anything put before him. His comprehension was not equal to his pronunciation, but it was far above average. However, the teacher says that he seemed to her to be nervous, and that many of his motor skills were below average. He had, for example, more difficulty in writing than most of the other children and his writing skills did not progress at a rate one would expect.

His mother agrees that his coordination has not been good, but she feels that it is improving now. She says that he gets along well with other children, but his teacher feels that this is not always true. The mother reports that Mark's favorite subject is arithmetic, and that he still wets the bed at times.

The psychologist's report is as follows:

> On the Wechsler Intelligence Scale for Children, Mark demonstrated a Verbal IQ of 113, a Performance IQ of 99, and a Full Scale IQ of 107. An analysis of the subtest scores indicates that Mark's general fund of information and ability to use verbal abstractions are high.
>
> His general judgment, comprehension, and ability to plan ahead are barely average. His ability to predict the behavior of other people is average. He is above

average in noting details and identifying missing elements. He is decidedly poor in maintaining sustained work activity.

The general impression from the Wechsler is that Mark is a bright boy, with particularly good academic aptitudes and average social intelligence who is emotionally relatively immature and dependent.

On the Wide Range Achievement Test, Mark demonstrated sight-reading at the 5.2 grade level and arithmetic at the 3.1 grade level. It is apparent that Mark's academic achievement, like his general fund of information, far exceeds what one would expect in terms of his general verbal intelligence. But his especially high ability to use verbal abstractions accounts in a large part for his advanced arithmetic achievement and particularly his excellent sight reading. It would seem that he is definitely bright academically and should plan for college, but his general judgment, comprehension and intellectual maturity are not as advanced as the specific paper-and-pencil school skills.

His drawings indicate some feelings of rejection, lack of confidence, and difficulty in maintaining sustained attention to the task at hand. Most of all, his drawings indicate intense feelings of frustration. These drawings indicate that Mark's home and school situation frustrates and blocks his attempts to find needed satisfaction. In short, he is an angry little boy who expends a lot of energy and mental effort holding his anger in check. The Rorschach reveals impulsivity as a result of sudden increases in anxiety. His energies are scattered and he has no available means for releasing anxieties along approved channels.

He is making a satisfactory identification with his father, but he is uncertain of his relationship with his father. He finds his relationship with his mother even

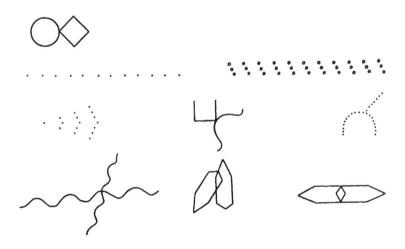

Figure 1. *Bender-Gestalt Designs. These are the standard Bender-Gestalt Designs. Each design is on a separate card, and each card is situated directly in front of the examinee as he draws. Thus, no recall is involved. The examinee is looking directly at each design as he draws it.*

© by Lauretta Bender and American Orthopsychiatric Association, Inc.

more difficult to satisfactorily work out. He feels pressure from his parents to achieve academically and socially more than he is able to do comfortably. He is having to devote too much of his time and energies in defending his ego. He is not happy nor is he able to lose himself in pleasant, productive play and work. Perhaps the pressures from his parents are subtle, but he feels them to be encroaching on every aspect of his life.

Because of his parents' obvious love for him, because they are motivated to do the best for him, he is unable to direct his anger toward them. Thus his aggression toward his parents and teachers is passive, namely, absent-mindedness, daydreaming, inefficiency, inattention, listlessness, and laziness. These are the ways he preserves his separate identity

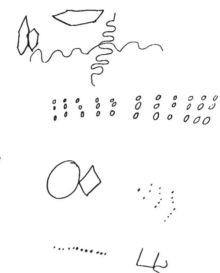

Figure 2.
*Mark W.'s Drawings of the
Bender Designs. Note that the
design in the extreme upper
left-hand corner of the page
(Design No. 7) is a mirror
image of the correct design
shown in Figure 1.*

from parents who press too close.

Conclusion: Passive-aggressive defenses in a bright boy with excellent academic aptitude and average social maturity. He has failed to develop adequate emotional maturity and independence, and devotes too much energy and mental effort in defending his ego from pressures by the parents.

The parents need help in realizing the ways they have blocked this boy from finding satisfactory outlets for anxiety and aggression, and for discovering ways to be independent. They need to begin immediately to find ways to allow this boy more independence, to let him take credit for his achievements, and allow him more control of his own life in areas that are primarily his.

Figure 3. *Mark W.'s Draw-A-Person.*

Discussions with Mr. and Mrs. W. concerning the pressures they, particularly the mother, were unwittingly applying led to a realistic re-evaluation of what they were doing and the effects these pressures were having on Mark.

Of course, it was not easy for Mrs. W. to realize that Mark would be much more the way she wanted him to be if she were more relaxed in her relationship with him. But Mr. W. quickly understood, actively helped in persuading Mrs. W., and promised he would work conscientiously to rectify the situation. Every effort was made to give Mrs. W. the emotional support she needed in order to view her maternal responsibilities in a new light.

By the time the discussions with the parents ended, Mrs. W. seemed completely accepting of the interpretations offered her, and although she was not sure that she could change as much as she would like, she planned to change as much as she could. Mr. and Mrs. W. were encouraged to emphatically recognize Mark's good behavior and to minimize criticism and pressure. The case was considered closed with the staff agreeing that the prognosis appeared good.

Six years later, a follow-up report was received from the public health nurse. It stated that Mark's mother *"has let him be independent."* Mark was described now as an *"A and B student,"* and *"will go into the 8th grade."*

David E.

David's parents feel that he has some problems and they hope that by seeking help they will keep these problems from becoming more serious. He is nearly eight years old and is in the second grade. His teacher informs us that in her opinion he is capable of doing average work at his grade level when left on his own. *"He is always the last in the room"*, she says, *"to finish his work, though far from being the least capable."* She describes David as being able to reason well and do well in verbal tasks. He is very slow in reading, but he understands what he reads. She feels that his *"slowness is due to immaturity and that pushing him might be harmful."*

Mr. and Mrs. E. both attended college, but neither graduated. The public health nurse describes them as *"very good parents, but perhaps a little over-protective."* They have another little boy four years of age. The relationships between the family seem good but the parents are apparently quite preoccupied with their children's growth and development. Mr. E. is the traffic manager for a large packing firm, likes his work and is considered successful in the eyes of the community.

David is described by his parents as being more advanced in many ways than other children his age. He has always talked more maturely than other children his age and seemed to understand better. But he has always been easily excitable and given to bedwetting and nightmares after hard play, and unless a firm stand is taken by the parents, he tends to be disobedient. He hates reading and doing homework. The public health nurse states that when she observes him, David appears shy and a little afraid in social situations. He has one very close friend and rarely plays with other children.

The psychologist describes David as a friendly, attractive "all American boy," full of vigor and vitality. Throughout the psychological testing, however, he worked slowly and methodically with frequent self-criticisms and showed other indications of lack of confidence. The psychologist's report is as follows:

> On the Wechsler Intelligence Scale for Children he obtained a Verbal IQ of 120, a Performance IQ of 101 and a Full Scale IQ of 112. His fund of general information, ability to use judgment in everyday

situations, and his ability to relate two concepts were considerably above the average for his age group. His slow and methodical approach to the test items handicapped him on the Performance Scale and it is possible that without this handicap, he would have scored even higher than the bright normal range of intelligence in which he is presently functioning.

There were some slight distortions in his Bender-Gestalt figures, but they appeared to be more the result of an emotional disturbance than of any visual-perceptual difficulty.

The Draw-A-Person figures indicated feelings of anxiety and insecurity in an emotionally immature individual. He is making an adequate attempt to contact others in his environment but it is a shallow attempt and he still feels isolated.

The Rorschach Test likewise indicated the strong feelings of anxiety and insecurity revealed by the Draw-A-Person Test. He has some mildly hostile impulses which are expressed through a passive negativism rather than through any overt expression of hostility.

He has some mildly depressive trends which probably stem from a feeling of being isolated. He has difficulty making effective interpersonal relationships. He is aware of other individuals but prefers to keep them at a psychological distance probably because he is distrustful of them.

There is a considerable creative potential which he is not utilizing at the present time. He appears to be utilizing so much energy in an attempt to control his impulses that he has little energy available for other activities.

On the Wide Range Achievement Test, David obtained a reading grade level of 2.1 and an arithmetic grade level of 2.7. These scores were slightly below his present grade placement.

The total test picture is that of an individual functioning in the bright normal range of intelligence but who appears to have an emotional disturbance characterized by anxiety, insecurity, and mild depressive trends.

The staff agreed that David's parents should be persuaded to reduce the pressure and let David become more independent. During the interpretive discussion with the parents, the findings and conclusions were fully presented to the parents. It was recommended, for example, that David be informed that in the future he must do his own homework, that his parents would help only when asked. Mr. and Mrs. E. seemed accepting of the recommendations and expressed appreciation for the evaluation.

They suggested that for three months they would attempt to alter their relationships with David, reduce the pressure and allow him to be more independent. If progress at the end of that time seemed good, they would continue to work along those lines. If not, they would return for further evaluations and discussions. They did not return.

Eight years later the public health nurse visited his school and home, and filed the following report: *"David E. is in the 10th grade going into the 11th. He has improved a lot and the parents followed all our suggestions. He is a fine boy!"* The last report received from the public health nurse stated simply, *"David E. graduated from high school; no problems."*

Scott K.

Scott was referred by a psychiatrist for psychological evaluation. He was reported to be doing poorly in school, and to have a "phobia" of school. He is fifteen years old and is in the ninth grade. Except for a report of a previous psychologist when he was twelve years old, no other history or background material was provided.

The report of the previous psychologist stated that *"he was direct and poised in making his responses,"* that his answers to the questions were *"unusually mature and thoughtful,"* and that when the tasks became difficult for him, he *"shifted abruptly from correct definitions to 'I don't know'."* The report stated that he demonstrated a Verbal IQ of 123, a Performance IQ of 107, and a Full Scale IQ of 117.

The following psychological report is such a classic description of an oppositional youth it is presented despite the fact that no follow-up information is available.

> On the Wechsler Intelligence Scale for Children, Scott demonstrated a Verbal IQ of 126, a Performance IQ of 121, and a Full Scale IQ of 126. Except for a momentary confusion on the Digit Span subtest, he would have obtained a Verbal IQ of 133, and a Full Scale IQ of 130. (Author's note: Scott did 6 digits backward, but only 4 forward.)
>
> On the Wide Range Achievement Test he demonstrated a reading grade level of 11.3, a spelling grade level of 9.8, and an arithmetic grade level of 11.0. Considering the fact that Scott is in the 9th grade, this level of academic achievement is impressive and in keeping with his general intelligence. The projectile material denotes a basically sound

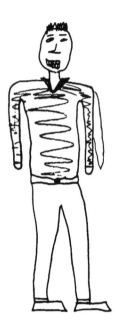

Figure 4. *Scott K.'s Draw-A-Person.*

personality with persistent anxiety concerning perfectionism. It appears that the interpersonal relationships within his family are warm and emotionally sound, but upward mobility places a stress on him. He feels that he is being pressured to achieve both socially and academically at a level beyond what he is capable of. He suffers from fears of loss of love if he does not come up to parental ambitions.

His younger siblings pose a threat to his position within the family, and he has no techniques for handling this except acting out emotionally or developing psychosomatic symptoms. This is the typical syndrome for what has sometimes been called a "school phobia," which in his case, because of his capacity for empathy, mature judgment and high intelligence, is a situational neurosis which could be alleviated by changes in parental treatment. He perceives his mother as both a source of threat and security and as a person preoccupied with finances. His father plays a more passive role in his thinking, and as a result he has difficulty in making a masculine identification.

Conclusion: Scott is a basically well-adjusted mature boy with maximum capacity to utilize his creativity and high intelligence, but is kept in a constant state of stress by an upwardly-mobile and dominating mother. His parents have met his basic emotional needs, but place demands for academic and social achievement which he feels are uncomfortable. He feels frustrated and threatened by his younger siblings.

Despite all this he is actually achieving academically at a maximum level. A slight lessening of pressure on him would be extremely beneficial. It is remarkable that the pressures applied to him happen to be exactly the maximum he can tolerate, and that he has just the amount of ego-strength needed to direct the resulting frustration and anxiety into constructive achievement. If he can continue to hold the present emotional balance, he probably will blossom when he gets out from under the home situation.

Chris F.

Chris attends a private school noted for its stress on high academic achievement and firm disciplinary standards. He is eight years old and is in the second grade, having repeated the first grade. The teacher reports that his school work is barely satisfactory, but she is certain that he will be promoted to the third grade. His mother is not sure that promoting him at this time is desirable. She feels that perhaps if he were retained in the second grade for another year he would be better prepared for third-grade work. Chris does fairly well in arithmetic, is poor in spelling, but reading is his major problem. He is easily distracted and has great difficulty in concentrating. His parents believe that he is intelligent, and that he has a good memory. They cannot understand why he does not do better in school. Chris is the youngest of three children. His older sisters do quite well in school.

Mrs. F. is a college graduate, and Mr. F., who is very successful in a skilled trade, feels that she, because of her better education, is better equipped to help Chris with his school work. And Mrs. F. has seen to it that Chris has plenty of educational materials accessible at home—books, records, films, etc. Chris is required to do his homework and get his lessons done before he is allowed any playtime at home.

Mr. F. readily admits that Mrs. F. is more of a disciplinarian than he. He states, however, that he does not have to discipline the children; they do what he wishes without it. Mrs. F. is something of a perfectionist, always busy, a dedicated homemaker whose activities center around her work, her home and her children. She has high expectations of her children's school performances and socialization abilities, especially Chris. And her expectations for Chris, according to her husband, are never met. She is always telling Chris that he could do better or that she expected him to do better.

Mr. F., however, believes that Chris *"can do anything he*

wants to do, or anything he has to do." He feels that Chris is just not interested in school, that he would rather play than work. He frequently takes the boy fishing and hunting, and Chris loves these activities. Mr. F. has promised to get Chris a horse if he passes his grade this year. Admittedly, he is disappointed in Chris as far as his school work is concerned, but he hopes that time will bring about a change if he and his wife keep pushing Chris.

At home, when not involved with school work, Chris is described as a healthy, happy, playful child. He makes friends with other children easily, engages in vigorous play activities, is not preoccupied with T.V., and gets along reasonably well with his sisters. He has no sleep disturbances, and is not afraid of the dark.

Chris was seen originally by the psychologist in the first grade during brief screening interviews at his school. The following is the psychologist's report following a complete evaluation at the clinic, Chris being at the time in the last half of the second grade:

> On the Wechsler Intelligence Scale for Children, Chris demonstrated a Verbal IQ of 95, a Performance IQ of 75, and a Full Scale IQ of 84. His verbal skills and knowledge appear average, but his judgment seems a little low. His non-verbal skills, however, appear poor, and this fact seems due to strong oppositional tendencies; anxiety, rigidity, and impulsivity which produce general confusion.
>
> The behavior on the Wechsler strongly suggests that his problems are due to subtle but pervasive parental pressures. Previous brief screening testing revealed relatively better judgment than he now shows;

this would be consistent with the hypothesis that he is potentially able to develop normal judgment, but is not doing so because of oppositionalism.

On the Wide Range Achievement Test, he demonstrated reading at the 2.1 grade level and arithmetic at the 2.5 grade level. He is in the second grade. Previous testing when he was in the first grade revealed reading at the 1.3 grade level and arithmetic at the 0.6 grade level. From these scores it appears that his school achievement and progress is fairly adequate.

His Draw-A-Person indicates some intellectual disturbance and immaturity, emotional constriction, and the feeling that he is being pressured to achieve more socially and academically than he comfortably can. His Bender drawings indicate frustration, impulsivity, and strong oppositional tendencies.

The Rorschach indicates rather pervasive emotional constriction and confusion. He is ambitious, but strongly oppositional. His relations with others are disturbed but he seems better able to relate to men than to either women or other children. He does not understand himself or the situation he is in, and is very near to being overwhelmed by the problems he faces.

Conclusion: oppositionalism, emotional constriction and confusion in a boy with normal intelligence. The primary cause of his difficulties appears to be subtle but pervasive parental pressures. But it appears also that inconsistency of treatment is complicating and confusing his efforts at adjustment. The parents need to have Chris' problems explained to them as clearly as possible.

In view of his present confusion and reaction to pressure, it seems he would much more likely find a chance to regain emotional stability and perspective in a public school; his present enrollment in a private school that is known to place great emphasis on

Figure 5.
Chris F.'s Bender Designs.

Started Design # 7 here,
but did not have enough
space to complete it...

...so he drew it over here.

Figure 6. *Chris F.'s Draw-A-Person.*

academic achievement certainly aggravates and magnifies his emotional problems. It must be emphasized that continuing the kinds of pressure that he is now subjected to will definitely lead to even more serious and disruptive emotional problems.

The psychological evaluation was discussed in detail with the parents. They were reassured to learn that there was nothing wrong with their son's intelligence. Mrs. F. acknowledged that she worked a great deal with Chris, but she was not conscious of exerting undue pressure on the child. Mr. F., for his part, was surprised that there could be any harm in pushing Chris.

It was pointed out to them that Chris felt pressure about his academic achievement both at home and at school. It was explained that Chris sees himself as a total failure as far as school is concerned. Although he is secretly ambitious, this will have little effect on his overt behavior unless he experiences some success. If whatever he does is never good enough, he will never become confident enough to really strive.

The parents were advised to let Chris get his lessons on his own, helping him only when he asked for help, and paying more attention to what he does well and correctly, than to what he does poorly or incorrectly. The mother said that she could do this, but she predicted that without her help and prodding his grades would go down. Again, it was reiterated how help and prodding may take away all feelings of success a child might have.

The whole problem of oppositionalism as a reaction to parental pressures was discussed at great length. If a child's grades go down, the parents were told, it should be because he has neglected his responsibilities, and if they go up it should be because of his own personal efforts. When we prod a child into success, we take away his pleasure in success.

The parents were reminded that Chris is now being prodded and pushed, and is achieving far below what he should be achieving. The more he is prodded, it would appear, the worse he does. Does it not make sense, the parents were asked, that Chris might actually be performing poorly as a reaction against this prodding and pushing? In fact, could not the fact that he acts at times as if he is mentally retarded be because he is unconsciously trying to get out from under the excessively high expectations his parents have for him? It was emphasized that Chris does not realize what he is doing, that he does not know any more than his parents do, why he performs poorly in school. All he knows, it was pointed out, is that he cannot seem to concentrate, understand, and remember as the other children do, that he hates school and is terribly depressed by the whole thing.

The parents gradually began to understand, the father first and then the mother. They said that they would have to talk about it and think about it before they decided what they felt they should do. They were assured that they could come back for further discussion, and that the public health nurse would keep in contact with them. They were advised to not interfere if the school promoted Chris to the third grade; and, regardless of whether he passes or not, to transfer him to a public school at the end of the year. The parents were warned that without the parental prodding and pushing Chris' grades may go down temporarily; they should view this as a test to see if they are really going to let Chris take charge of his life.

The staff was not certain what the outcome might be. If Chris' problems were to be alleviated, the mother was going to have to change some strongly held convictions about her role. However, follow-up contacts were encouraging. Chris passed on schedule into the third grade and his parents transferred him to a public school. The last report received from the public health nurse came two years later: *"Mrs. F. is still a perfectionist, but she seems to have relaxed quite a bit in regard to Chris' school work; Chris is doing good work in the public school; no problems."*

Steve D.

Steve is twenty-four years old. He is well-dressed in a suit and tie. He was referred by a psychiatrist in private practice to whom he had originally gone because of his problem. He is seen by the psychologist as a private client and pays for the evaluation himself. He states that he is employed as a salesman for new and used automobiles. He states that he is able to make a good living at this occupation, has done so for several years, and supports a wife and two children. His problem, he says, is that he cannot read nor write, and he wants to know why. The only history obtained is related in the psychologist's report, and no follow-up information is available. The case is presented in order to show a possible consequence of oppositionalism in an elementary school child. The psychologist's report is as follows:

Mr. Steve D. states that he has only an elementary education, that he was terminated in elementary school because he could not read and spell. He reports a history of brain injury, but states that his academic difficulties existed before the injury.

On the Wechsler Adult Intelligence Scale, he demonstrates a Verbal IQ of 119, a Performance IQ of 108, and a Full Scale IQ of 115. His judgment tests superior, and his abilities to abstract verbally and to identify logical detail errors are high. His form perception and non-verbal reasoning are above average. His fund of information, immediate recall, and social intelligence are average. Only his speed at routine paper-and-pencil tasks is well below average. There is absolutely no evidence of brain damage on the

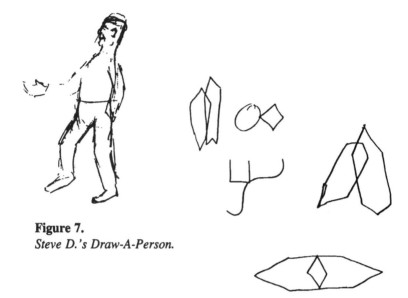

Figure 7.
Steve D.'s Draw-A-Person.

Figure 8. *Steve D.'s Bender Designs.*

Wechsler, nor any other weaknesses revealed on the Wechsler that would account for his failure to learn to read.

On the Wide Range Achievement Test, he demonstrated reading at the 7.1 grade level, spelling at the 3.6 grade level, and arithmetic at the 4.8 grade level.

His Draw-A-Person reveals some affectional anxiety (fear of loss of love), and some talent for drawing. The Bender drawings reveal outgoing aggressiveness but no marked hostility, and nothing else significant. On the Memory-for-Designs Test, a test for brain damage, he obtained a raw score of 0, and a difference score of 0; high scores on this test indicate brain damage; thus, his scores indicate that no brain damage is present.

The Rorschach indicates good reality ties, but difficulty in relating to others. He has made a fairly good masculine identification and is comfortable in the masculine role. But from early childhood, he has failed to relate to others, and this failure is associated with intense emotionality and acting out. He is sexually responsive and uses sex as a primary source of emotional stability, but he is strongly oppositional (stubborn, negativistic, "hard-headed") in his relations with women (and his mother). It would seem that as a child he was a conduct problem and acted out his emotional needs without regard to, or in opposition to, his mother (and other female adults). He is not now ambitious, but is primarily concerned with holding to what he now has. He attempts to find expression in some artistic field (music or art?), but he has difficulties in integrating his emotional reactions with his behavior. In his dealings with others, he is spontaneous, impulsively outgoing and talkative.

Conclusion: In general, there seems to be no neurological nor psychological factor which could account for Mr. D.'s poor academic skills. Whatever event or series of events which resulted in his failings to develop academic skills, and one could postulate several different possibilities, at present there is no reason why he could not acquire at least average reading, writing, and arithmetic skills. Although he certainly has anxieties about it, and will experience set-backs when under stress, if he is motivated to do so, he could with or without a tutor, accomplish his goals in these areas.

Eric B.

Eric B. was referred because he is *"unable to learn in school."* He is eleven years old, the oldest of three children, and is in the fifth grade, having repeated the second grade. He gets along well with his classmates and teachers, but the quality of his school work is described as "poor."

Eric's father is a skilled mechanic, but did not graduate from high school. His mother went only as far as the ninth grade. Mr. and Mrs. B. described Eric as a very emotional child, easily disturbed by things that do not bother other children. But he socializes well, plays on the basketball team, and is active in the Boy Scouts.

The psychological report on Eric B. is as follows:

> On the Wechsler Intelligence Scale for Children, Eric demonstrated a Verbal IQ of 95, a Performance IQ of 85, and a Full Scale IQ of 89. In general, he was slow and hesitant on the Wechsler, but he behaved in a normally intelligent way.
>
> His speed at routine paper-and-pencil tasks is extremely slow, but his judgment is a little above average and he shows an average fund of information, average immediate recall, and an average ability to identify logical detail errors. His form perception, ability to plan ahead, and carry out plans are also average. He has a little difficulty keeping himself from making impulsive errors, and this probably accounts for why he is so slow at routine paper work. He is a little below average in understanding verbal abstractions and his social intelligence tested low.
>
> He seems suspicious and distrustful of adults, and was generally passive and unresponsive during the

testing. He seemed listless, uncommunicative, and was not spontaneous. He did not seem motivated to do his best on the various test items, and his approach was rather casual and haphazard. Toward the end of the testing session, however, he gradually became more responsive, spontaneous, and motivated.

On the Wide Range Achievement Test, he demonstrated reading at the 4.0 grade level and arithmetic at the 4.2 grade level. He is in the fifth grade. His Bender drawings are fairly accurate, but seem rather haphazardly drawn. His Draw-A-Person was immaturely drawn (he drew a female figure), and the way it is drawn indicates emotional constriction and a general feeling on his part that he is being pressured to achieve more socially and educationally than he comfortably can.

The Rorschach indicates good reality ties, but a general inability to cope with life in general. He feels that people are against him and he has not developed broad interests primarily because he must use so much of his mental energies to hold people at a distance. He is frustrated and must maintain strong curbs on his own behavior in order to prevent impulsive acting out. He is surprisingly still ambitious, but he views his world as harsh and he is reluctant to let others find out his ambitions.

He is comfortable in the masculine role, but has not been able to make a sound masculine identification. He is oppositional, negativistic, depressed, and frustrated, and is unable to relate to either other children or adults in a trusting, emphatic way. He is a lonely, isolated person who finds few rewards from life.

Conclusions: Normal intelligence with some losses in intellectual functioning due to subtle but strong parental pressures. He is somewhat behind in school

Figure 9. *Eric B.'s Draw-A-Person.*

achievement, and his personal ambition is generally inhibited. He apparently has not been allowed to achieve independently and gain rewards for this achievement; and thus he finds little pleasure in achievement and his main motivation is aimed at defending what little independence he has. Parental counseling is recommended.

The social worker's report of the interpretative interview with Mr. and Mrs. B. concerning Eric's evaluation is as follows:

Mr. and Mrs. B. were seen by the psychologist and social worker for interpretation of psychological findings and assistance with planning.

Positives were pointed out in both child and parents prior to getting down to the crux of the problem. The psychologist initially related to the parents that Eric's difficulty is one that is seen often but is always easy to solve. Parents can usually help a great deal but some readjustment is required. Recognition was given to the good intentions of the parents but emphasis was placed on the fact that these sometimes backfire. Understandably, the parents have high expectations of their only son, but subtle and pervasive parental pressure is at the base of much of his difficulty.

Consultants further explained that Eric is ambitious but his ambition is well guarded and the fun of achieving for its own sake is absent. Eric is dragging his heels and going through the motions and doing whatever he does for others' enjoyment rather than his own. He is depressed, unhappy, frustrated. It was pointed out that Eric hasn't learned to enjoy achieving at school and he needs to have an opportunity to try things out, make mistakes and deal with the world himself. He is mechanically inclined and does a great deal of experimenting on his own and he should be allowed to go at his own pace.

Mother inquired as to why Eric does the opposite of what she wants him to do. The psychologist acknowledged that Eric is negativistic and oppositional and explained that he tries to maintain his own self-identity in the face of the fact that he receives very little personal reward and encouragement. Eric needs to feel that he counts and what he wants to do matters rather than having to use all of his energy trying to keep from being angry all the time. Reassurance was given concerning the presence of normal intellectual ability. Eric is sort of turned into himself and doesn't get enough fun out of life. Considerable time was spent discussing the method of successive approximation (rewarding his best efforts) and emphasis placed on the necessity for parental reward for his small achievements.

Father seemed emphatic and redirected discussion back to school and the problem developing there. The psychologist asserted that the pattern was already there when he started school. He went on to say that the parents' tendency to be too concerned has resulted in the boy dragging his heels in most areas of his life. Mr. B. sought further explanation for Eric's lack of ability to make decisions. Seemingly, he looks to his parents for what they want him to do. The psychologist assured him that this is not Eric's problem, but rather that the parents are going to have to change.

Both parents indicated sincere interest in Eric and seemed confident about what they may be able to do with this increased understanding of their role and contribution to the child's problem. Mother readily accepted the suggestion that she come back and talk to the social worker next month as we would be interested to know how they were getting along.

Six weeks later the mother met again with the social worker. The latter's summary of this final discussion is as follows:

Mrs. B. focused on Eric and his school difficulties. Actually she can't see much change in Eric, but parents understand change will come gradually. They feel they are, with help they received here, on the right track now and are determined to continue their efforts.

Eric didn't pass and will repeat fifth grade next year. He was terribly disappointed and cried and cried. Parents were disappointed too, but more or less expected it. Mother admittedly found it extremely hard not to push Eric the last six weeks of school because she feared he would fail otherwise, but Mr. B. lent full support and reassured her that they must let him fail or make it on his own just like the psychologist said.

Eric is going to summer school hopefully to learn how to read and understand what he reads an hour each day. He is also provided with Weekly Readers and trips to the library. Mrs. B. said he likes to do everything but read and we thought perhaps he may learn to like to read since he is in a very small class and can go pretty much at his own pace. Eric also wants to go camping with the Scouts this summer. He spends his time riding his bike, fixing the lawnmower, camping out every now and then, crawfishing and spending a lot of time with one friend about his age. He played basketball on the first string and, though nervous, did quite well. We believe that this has helped him to gain a little more self-confidence with his peers and in his own ability.

Attention then turned back to school and plans for the fall. Obviously, Mrs. B. is still very much involved with their child's school achievement. She has already requested that Eric is placed in a different class as he did not like his teacher last year, and she wants him to have a different one.

This interview was largely supportive of parental efforts with regard to change in management. Mrs. B. understands that we are interested and agreed to call and give us a report or come in and talk again if new problems arise.

She did not return. Three years later Eric is in the seventh grade. His mother is described as having changed very little. His teacher says that Eric is a *"weak student who always does his homework and who tries to learn."* He is shy and timid, with only a few close friends. It appears that despite her efforts to change, Mrs. B. is still applying pervasive pressures and Eric is still reacting oppositionally to them. For Eric, chronic underachievement (see next chapter) seems to have become his new habitual technique for dealing with parental pressures.

CHAPTER 5

Chronic Underachievers

Children who begin school with fully developed and stabilized patterns of oppositionalism are very likely to have specific academic difficulties. These difficulties can become new weapons to use in the emotional tug-of-war with their parents. Children constantly criticized at home and pressured to achieve more socially and academically than they feel able frequently discover at school techniques of simulated stupidity which exasperate teachers and which, when manifested at home, are equally disturbing to parents.

It should not be surprising that this happens. Burdened with anxiety and self-doubt, frustrated wherever he turns, the child who is made to feel inadequate at home is in fact frequently unable to concentrate in school. While the teacher is explaining the lessons, he is usually preoccupied with his emotional problems, and his attention is turned inward. When assigned academic work to do, he often sits and stares blankly at the book or paper. If he does any work at all it will be at a painfully slow pace with frequent halts, errors, irrelevances, and corrections. The teacher who observes this may realize that the child has some sort of "emotional block" which is preventing him from learning, but usually there is little she can do to overcome it. Not infrequently the teacher becomes increasingly convinced that the child is dull or even mentally retarded.

In any case, most teachers realize that criticizing or pressuring such a child will do no good, and the teacher may try to convince the parents of this. But because the child's school achievement is so poor, the teacher unfortunately is prone to encourage the parents to require him to do more studying at home, which sets the stage for increased parent-child conflicts. Thus the anxieties of the teacher may feed parental anxieties and create for the already overwhelmed child additional conditions of stress.

Under these circumstances, the child is even less able to concentrate on what he is supposed to be learning. The conclusion that he is mentally limited or deficient, or that he simply is unable to learn to read, spell or do arithmetic soon seems unavoidable.

One or both of the parents may continue for a while to urge the child to do better, but usually everyone concerned, including the child himself, gradually comes to accept his specific academic ineptitude or general dullness as fact. Since a lack of inherent ability is perfectly acceptable as a reason for academic failings, this conclusion may finally even be welcomed by the parents, teachers, and especially by the child. Having been accused repeatedly of being lazy, absent-minded, obstinate, and willfully inattentive, with everyone now agreeing that he simply cannot learn the way the other children do, the Oppositional Child is in a far less vulnerable position.

If he is bright, as nearly all oppositional children are, he then proceeds to develop an elaborate repertoire of tricks to keep the significant adults in his life convinced that he is really striving to cooperate and study. With his mind a thousand miles away, he learns to bend over his papers and books in a posture of deep concentration. He may shape the words he is reading with his mouth, whisper to himself, or mumble, frown, and hold the paper up to the light. Without listening to a word, he can appear exceedingly attentive when someone says something to him and, without losing the thread of the fantasies he is preoccupied with, politely ask that it be repeated.

His halting way of talking and reading, with frequent apologies or uncertainties, and his slow way of writing, with frequent erasures or cross outs, become habitual. The whole pattern of intellectual and academic obtuseness, originally the result of an emotional preoccupation, is developed into a fine art and used skillfully to ward off further attacks on his self-esteem.

Not fully aware of what is happening, but grateful for the means of lessening criticism and pressure, the child who successfully conceals his true abilities from his parents and teachers deprives them of their main reasons for being concerned about him. The parents are thus relieved of the responsibility for his poor school achievement, and his teachers can lower their expectations.

Periodically, new efforts may be launched to overcome his more serious weaknesses. But since he nearly always reacts to these efforts by performing even more poorly, they become less frequent as the years go by. Finally, the child is left to dawdle and daydream away his days in school convinced that he is a dullard, and considered so by his parents, teachers, siblings and peers.

He is now a fully developed chronic underachiever. No one chides him anymore with the admonition that if he would just apply himself he could do better. His difficulties with reading, writing or arithmetic are taken for granted. As he falls further behind he is not expected ever to catch up, and even less to excel.

The intellectual and academic handicaps of the chronic underachiever make his struggles for maturation and independence more difficult. Although his academic weaknesses may be confined to specific areas, there emerges in the child an image of himself as generally inadequate intellectually. He may be quite competent, even brilliant, in areas unrelated to school achievement, but he doggedly refuses to believe that what he possesses is the kind of intelligence needed for academic work.

Yet he is his parents' child, and has been imbued with their values and yearnings. No matter how much he may disparage those who are intellectually gifted, he in fact envies them. And in fantasy he will dream of intellectual attainments for himself, and may in secret actually carry on diligent but chaotic and disjointed programs of self-study. Burdened as he is, however, with what will probably be life-long feelings of inferiority, it may be many years before he risks disclosing to others his intellectual aspirations.

Chronic underachievers, although bright, typically score low or erratic on tests of intelligence. Patterns of induced dullness are sometimes so pervasive and entrenched that even experienced psychologists may be fooled by them. And when the dynamics are manifestly obvious, it is seldom an easy task to persuade parents that their child is not as dull as they think. Usually the parents report a history of low scores on IQ tests, which take precedence in their thinking over the opinion of what they may view as a well-meaning, but sadly misguided, psychologist.

What is difficult for parents to understand is that it is not necessary for them to have definite ideas about their children's ultimate capabilities. In fact, it is very likely to be harmful when they do. If they get the idea a child is bright, they are prone to pressure him and be dissatisfied with his achievement; if they think he is dull, they subtly undermine his confidence and thus set limits on what he will attempt.

The task of parents is to respond positively whenever their child makes a special effort to achieve. They should be ready to share with him his pride in small accomplishments. They should help the child identify his strengths, and should not feel compelled to criticize him or discourage him when he attempts something difficult. When he is not progressing as they would like, or when he seems to be retrogressing, they should be patient. Instead of blaming him for his failings, his parents should help him understand that in the major undertakings of life progress seldom runs smoothly.

Parents who can sympathize with their child when he feels inadequate or stupid, and who can rejoice with him in his successes, will have no need of knowing his level of capabilities. For the child of such parents will be what educators and psychologists call an "overachiever," that is, a child who succeeds beyond our expectations. Unless a child is severely handicapped mentally, and sometimes even when this is true, no one can say how far he may go with proper support and encouragement at home. The confident, eager-to-learn child is soon "over the fence and gone" as far as academic achievement is concerned, and since he functions so far ahead of his tested intelligence there is little practical utility in parents knowing how his IQ compares with others.

By the same token, parents who feel it is their duty to point out to their child his every mistake and who believe that they must stay after him or he will waste his time and talents will have little need to know their child's ultimate capabilities. For the child of such parents will seldom realize his full potentialities. It matters little that if he applied himself he could make straight A's. For he will never apply himself. At least he will never apply himself long enough or intensely enough to realize his true potentialities.

The school, however, whose job it is to actually do the teaching, may need to know how children compare with each other in terms of skills and ability. The school's task is to place children in classes where the materials, procedures, and tempo are conducive to learning. When a bright underachiever is held back it is almost always harmful to him, for quick learners seldom profit from slow-paced teaching. Slow learners, on the other hand, may need to be held back.

Furthermore, many chronic underachievers are in fact not underachievers at all. While displaying a paucity of knowledge and skills in the classroom, in what they have learned they may actually be up with their classmates or even ahead of them. There are others, however, who will have to break through their pattern of oppositionalism before they can come up to the level of their class.

When teachers and school officials are accurately aware of a child's abilities, of what he has and has not learned, and of the reasons he is not progressing satisfactorily in school, they can usually find ways to alleviate the difficulties. And this is especially true if they can gain the cooperation of his parents.

The need, therefore, is for tests and diagnostic instruments which effectively identify real strengths and weaknesses of students, and which accurately reveal the types of problems they are having.

Currently popular tests of intelligence, aptitude, and achievement, with their heavy reliance on time limits and total scores, often do a better job of concealing than of revealing children's true capabilities and knowledge. Since all a child has to do to fail one of these tests is to work slowly and leave questions unanswered, it should not be surprising that underachievers may score as low or lower than children with far less ability. Bright children who are predisposed toward failure will very likely fail whenever the means for failing are so obviously available to them.

Psychological forces within bright children, however, prevent them from being totally sluggish and inept when tested. For example, they frequently ask astute questions or are aware of incidental facts that dull children are oblivious to. They may reveal levels of reading comprehension higher than could be accounted for in terms of the scores they make on vocabulary tests. One might ask himself how, unless the child is especially skilled and stimulated academically, could he possibly comprehend what he reads at a level significantly above his vocabulary.

Unless they are bright, how is it that many are able to read difficult words while they are seemingly unable to read much easier ones? While correctly multiplying or dividing, how can they make mistakes in simple addition and subtraction? The test papers of bright underachievers frequently have answers in the wrong places, many questions left unanswered, and are unfinished. But if these children's abilities are judged in terms of what they do rather than in terms of what they leave undone, their test papers are often gold mines of useful diagnostic information. When tested individually, psychologists find that many chronic underachievers become so interested in what they are doing that they lose for the moment their habitual self-defeating behaviors, and on particular tests or subtests reveal remarkably high ability.

However, bright children who have successfully convinced everyone concerned that they are dull or limited in some specific way are seldom referred for psychological evaluation. Ordinarily no one sees any particular need for them to be seen by a psychologist. When they are seen, which is rare, they may reveal high abilities on individually administered tests of intelligence.

They are prone to score high on untimed tests of judgment and abstract reasoning, being more inclined to do poorly on timed tests or tests of academic skills. Although they may manifest some of the characteristics of oppositionalism, namely, drawing square bodies (with flat heads!), being slow in responding, refusing to guess or to say they don't know, etc., the fact that they effectively use feigned dullness to avoid parental pressures accounts for why they are usually distraught emotionally, as are most oppositional children.

Of course they are always burdened with intense feelings of inferiority and consider themselves hopeless academically, but they commonly seem to accept such things philosophically and even light-heartedly, without overwhelming anxiety, depression, or hostility. This is true, that is, if the parents are still prevailing on them to do better.

Under such circumstances, they may perform uniformly poorly on all tests of intelligence and they may manifest typical oppositional emotional disturbance in drawings and on the Rorschach. To make correct diagnoses, the psychologist must be alert for informal and fortuitous signs of hidden ability.

Until the appearance of the long-awaited improvements needed in tests of ability and achievement, professional educators should follow the lead of those psychologists who place more emphasis on what children do than on the total scores they obtain on standardized tests. If we are to salvage the intellectual productivity of chronic underachievers, we must systematically search out their academic strengths and reinforce them, and not allow ourselves to be misled by seemingly inexorable scores on tests.

Because of parental pressures, some bright children may never acquire the rudimentary skills of reading, writing, spelling or arithmetic. But for every bright student who completely fails to acquire essential academic skills, there are hundreds who are functioning at the minimal level necessary for barely getting by, convinced that they are not capable of doing any better.

To deal effectively with the problem of underachievement, parents must first understand how the mechanisms of underachievement may be learned as instrumental defenses against parental criticisms or unreasonably high parental expectations. Chronic underachievers avoid parental pressures and alleviate their own feelings of guilt by convincing others and becoming convinced themselves that they are in some way dull or mentally limited. Once low achievement has become an established pattern, parents ordinarily do not harass the child about his poor school work. They make it abundantly clear to him that they do not do so only because of their belief in his low ability. He is therefore put on warning never to let them suspect that he has higher ability than he demonstrates.

The parents of underachievers typically fall into three camps: (1), those that continue to harass and criticize their children for their failings; (2), those that have washed their hands of the whole business; and (3), those who in some perverse way are able to do both these things simultaneously. Probably nothing so clearly conveys to the child his parents' combined disapproval, disinterest, and low opinion of him than the subtle rebuke which so often is used ostensibly to encourage the underachiever; namely, "As long as you are doing the best you can, that is all anyone can expect of you."

In confronting the parents of a bright underachiever, the psychologist is in something of a predicament. He knows that in all too many cases the greatest harm he can do the child is to convince the parents he is not dull or mentally limited. Parents often say that what they want to know is whether they should push their child or not, the implication being that if he is not bright then it is all right to let him dawdle. Rarely are they prepared to institute the kinds of support and encouragement that would actually help the child begin to use his abilities.

It is in their successful escape from parental pressures that chronic underachievers have such a distinct advantage over other types of oppositional children. And psychologists often feel reluctant to deprive them of this avenue of escape.

The earlier and the more thoroughly parental pressures are removed, the better the chances are the oppositional children will abandon their self-defeating patterns of failure. When convinced that their child is normally bright, many parents place insatiable demands on him. Nothing he ever does is good enough. His little successes are ignored and his major ones are taken for granted. When he has difficulties they are dismayed, and when he fails they feel bitterly betrayed. Such a child may be thirty or forty years old before he can finally think of himself as just an ordinary person who must struggle and work to achieve something of value in life. And ordinarily he must fail abysmally before he overcomes his oppositional reactions toward his parents. It is therefore often better to let parents go on underestimating their child's ability than to tell them something which they may interpret as justification for instituting increased pressure.

The chronic underachiever has thus obtained a distinct advantage over other types of pressured children. In failing his parents early he has in a way freed himself of them. Having given up on him, his parents cannot later lay claim to what he does accomplish. While other oppositional children remain so terrified of failure that they may never in their lives risk applying themselves, the chronic underachiever fails at the outset. Having disappointed his parents from the first, he does not fear disappointing them again.

The parents of the chronic underachiever are given the chance to gradually adapt to him as a failure, and he in turn can learn to live with this image of himself. Convinced that he is not as bright as others, he is not ashamed to have to work harder than they do. He expects to fail and of course nearly always does.

But with great reserves of unused intellectual ability, and with strong predispositions to compensate for intense feelings of inferiority, the chronic underachiever is psychologically primed to achieve. Sooner or later he will get at least some meager recognitions, and these recognitions will fall like rain on parched ground. Whatever he does to receive them, he will very likely repeat. Under the stimulation of a good teacher in high school or college he may blossom. And if he does, nobody will be more surprised than his parents, who paradoxically will continue to think of him as a failure long after he is clearly a success in the eyes of the world.

Unfortunately the first recognitions that many chronic non-achievers receive are in socially undesirable activities. The leaders or "brains" of most juvenile gangs are typically bright youths who have a long history of school failures. More fortunate are those who gain their first recognitions in sports, art or music. In many cases, these underachievers are drawn back into academic pursuits, as are those whose first real accomplishments occur in after-school jobs or in the military.

Although burdened for life with intense feelings of inferiority and handicapped intellectually by faulty academic skills (compared to other children who have been pressured too much by their parents), the chronic underachiever is in an enviable position. He at least can achieve. He can surprise everyone and make something of himself.

On the other hand, the pressured child who everyone believes is bright can only fail; maneuvered into a superiority role, and thus riddled with guilt and anxiety because he feels he can never come up to parental expectations, he is in the more tragic situation. And more tragic still are the instrumentally immature child and the pseudo-mature child, to be discussed later, who because of their early acquired patterns of reaction toward their parents will very likely never enjoy intimate, reciprocal relationships with others.

And unlike other types of oppositional children, the chronic underachiever can become achievement-oriented easily. He waits discouraged and depressed only for circumstance to reveal his hidden assets. Sooner or later this is bound to happen, and when it does his abilities and energies are loosed for productive achievement. His achievements may be informal, unconventional, and outside the mainstream of educational procedures, and, as has been mentioned before, unfortunately may occur in illegal or criminal pursuits.

As an adult he may feel out of place in most intellectual circles, and, as part of his effort to compensate for his feelings of inferiority, he may be particularly intolerant and impatient with the shortcomings of those he assumes to be "intellectuals." He very likely will resent the many opportunities he sees open to those without his educational and social handicaps, and will begrudge them their seemingly easy successes.

But paradoxically he will be as proud of his early academic failings and shortcomings as he is of his successes. He will view himself as a "self-made man" who had to overcome both personal inadequacies and obstacles placed in his path by those who underestimated his abilities, strength of will, and determination.

Most chronic underachievers do in some way or other succeed in life and, despite their feelings of inferiority, at maturity take ample pride in their accomplishments. Unfortunately, unless they have in the meantime gained some perspective about themselves, they become hard taskmasters as parents and are prone, in turn, to pressure their own children as they were pressured, thus perpetuating for another generation all the senseless and unnecessary evils of oppositionalism.

Illustrative Case
Kenneth T.

Kenneth T. is nearly nine years old, is in the third grade, and seems to have a "mental block" in reading. He repeated the first grade. His father, a high school graduate, is an estimator in an automotive repair shop. His mother, although not at present employed, is a registered nurse, a graduate of a two-year nursing program. He has an older brother and younger sisters. One of his younger sisters is in the same grade that he is in and is doing very well in school, as are his brother and other sister. When he started first grade he was put in the "fast" reading group, but began to go down immediately. He is in the "slow" reading group now and cannot read words that he was able to read in the first grade.

When reading he changes the wording, yet it contains the same thought. His attention span is short. His mother fears that there may be some mental "unbalance" present. He is moody, but plays well with other children, although, if he can, he avoids competitive sports.

On the playground he likes to be the leader and center of attention, and is something of a clown. His teacher states that his only problem is reading. *"He is able to sound words, prompt others, but when called on to read, he seems to face a blankness. He begs to read, because of such a desire to do better, but has the same problem again."*

Figure 10. *Kenneth T.'s Draw-A-Person.*

The psychological report on Kenneth is as follows:

On the Wechsler Intelligence Scale for Children, Kenneth demonstrated a Verbal IQ of 99, a Performance IQ of 103, and a Full Scale IQ of 101. All of his specific abilities are good, and his judgment and ability to reason abstractly are excellent. His reaction time and speed of motor-perceptual responses are average.

On the Wide-Range Achievement Test, his sight reading is at the 3.4 grade level, and his arithmetic is at the 3.5 grade level. Considering the fact he is in the third grade, these scores indicate no academic retardation in comparison with his grade mates, and considering his IQ, his academic achievement is about what would be expected. He reads very slowly, however, and he seems to be very hesitant in reading. If one does not grow impatient with him or conclude that because he is so slow in responding that he cannot read, he reads quite adequately for his grade level.

His drawings indicate shyness, constriction, lack of confidence, and some ambivalent aggression. Also in his drawings are indications that he feels academically "stupid" and that he feels pressured by parents and teachers to achieve more socially and academically than he comfortably can do.

The Rorschach indicates some difficulties in making a masculine identification, but there is evidence that he is overcoming this problem. He feels that others are against him, and that they are trying to block and frustrate him. He shows passive-negativism as his main defense against what he views as an unfriendly and stressful environment.

Conclusion: Kenneth is a normal child emotionally and intellectually, who uses passive-negativism as a defense against external threat and pressure. He views himself as academically "stupid." Parental counseling aimed at getting his parents to concentrate on rewarding him for what he does that is good, and allowing him to develop more responsibility without pressuring him is recommended.

His reading is extremely slow, not because he cannot read nor because his reaction time is slow, but as an involuntary delaying tactic against pressure. Not letting this device bother the teacher or the parents, letting him read at whatever rate of speed he wishes, should overcome this specific problem. The parents should not tutor him in his reading. They should provide him with reading materials, take an interest in whatever he reads, but not correct or rush him.

Mrs. T. was seen by the psychologist and the social worker to discuss the psychological findings and recommendations. Mrs. T. began the session by reiterating that Kenneth's teacher says that he cannot read. She said that she devotes time to coaching and drilling him, and expresses dissatisfaction with the results on trial tests. She stated that she regrets not having worked with him more in the past. She described Kenneth as being absent-minded and easily disturbed. She was firm in her belief that Kenneth needs special help or he will never learn to read.

The psychologist's initial explanation to the mother was that Kenneth's reading difficulties are not due to any real lack of ability, but rather is a device he uses to reduce parental pressure. The mother denied that she had pressured the child, but feels strongly that she should do so now. The mother stated that Kenneth had difficulty in the first grade in adjusting to school, and ever since then his reading has become worse. Mrs. T. emphatically rejected the idea of excessive parental pressures. The psychologist agreed that the pressures were perhaps subtle and unintentional on the parents' part, but he demonstrated from the test results and from what had been said about the child that Kenneth felt pressured.

The mother suggested that perhaps Kenneth is under excessive "self-pressure," and that perhaps she has conveyed to the child some of her own attitudes and values regarding education and the need to conscientiously do well whatever has to be done. The psychologist agreed that this is very likely what has happened, and efforts must be made to help Kenneth discover the rewards that can be gained from achievement, and his failures to achieve should not be emphasized.

The mother should show constructive interest but not concern. It was suggested to the mother that she should provide the child with attractive and appropriate reading materials, be responsive whenever the child shows an interest in reading, but essentially refrain from taking on any aspect of instructing the child in reading. The mother stated that the child simply cannot concentrate, and if not drilled at home will surely fail in school. The psychologist assured the mother that Kenneth is perfectly capable of concentrating, and when he discovers more pleasure in achieving in school than in failing he will progress quite well.

From his mother he needs emotional support, not instruction on how to read. The interview was concluded with clarification that progress may be slow, that there are many little things that have to be changed, and that setbacks will occur, but if the emphasis at home will be on helping Kenneth find pleasure in his school work and gain confidence in his abilities, in a few years his academic achievement will be all the parents could desire.

The staff was not too sure Mrs. T. would follow its advice. But follow-up discussions with her by the public health nurse revealed encouraging possibilities. Mrs. T. seemed to be relaxing the pressure on Kenneth. She had gone back to work and was no longer helping him with his reading.

The last follow-up report was received four years later: *"Kenneth was passed to the 8th grade, but is attending summer school for one subject failed. All his other grades are B's and C's."*

CHAPTER 6

Patterns of Superficial Regression: The Instrumentally Immature

Some children under constant criticism and disapproval do not engage in a contest of wills with their parents, but rather seem to surrender completely to parental pressures. These children, long before they start to school, retreat into patterns of superficial regression as a means of avoiding parental pressures and as a way of obtaining at least some short-term psychological gratifications. Unlike simple, uncomplicated oppositional children who slowly progress toward maturity and achievement despite elaborate patterns of procrastination and evasion, and unlike chronic underachievers who restrict their recalcitrance to failings in the school and classroom, these oppositional children seem to pursue a course of psychological self-annihilation, a pervasive denial of their true emotional and intellectual inclinations and potential.

Like all oppositional children, superficially regressive

children effectively frustrate their parents' fondest hopes, but at a price far above that which other oppositional children pay. Children who use superficial regression as their main defense against parental tyrannies typically appear much more disturbed than other types of oppositional children. The fact is they usually are much more disturbed, but not in the ways they appear to be.

Instrumental immaturity is the most common form of superficial regression. As a defense against parental pressures, the instrumentally immature have simply learned to act a great deal more immature than they actually are. There is, of course, little that parents can demand of children who convincingly behave as if they lack normal emotional control and intellectual capacity. And immaturity is such an easy thing for bright children to fake. Being as it is such a formidable defense against parental pressures, and so easy to fake, it is perhaps surprising that not more pressured children feign immaturity.

Be that as it may, what is not so surprising is that once patterns of feigned immaturity become relied upon as children's habitual defenses against overzealous parents, it is usually very difficult to break up these patterns and get the children to risk acting maturely. It is as if they realize that the moment they drop their facades of "babyishness," Mommy and Daddy will pounce on them and overwhelm them with their insatiable demands.

Instrumentally immature children can be the bane of their parents' existence, always having problems, always sick and whiny, and forever accusing their parents of not loving them. Such children cling to their mother as if they are terrified of the world. They can pucker up and cry real tears at the slightest provocation. And when asked even the simplest question they characteristically drop their mouths open and stare as if they lacked ordinary common sense. They easily fall into the role of family scapegoat, and are fussed at and nagged at, not only by the parents, but by the older and younger siblings as well.

The tragedy is that, once acquired, the instrumentally immature's patterns of behavior eventually are carried over into their relationships with children and adults outside of the family, and sooner or later effectively cripple their capacity to form any mature reciprocal friendships.

When finally out from under parental control, the instrumentally immature typically seek others who will play the role of the harassing parents and siblings. As adults they are drawn into webs of social involvements where they feel unloved, rejected and "ugly." They typically marry inadequate, unfeeling persons who treat them even more harshly than their families did.

They become lonely, isolated people who are an emotional burden to those around them, yet who constantly gain special privileges for themselves because of their obvious weaknesses, helplessnesses or illnesses. They feel that they are exploited, which of course they are, but they seduce people into taking advantage of them because this is the only role they know how to play and is the only way they can be involved in the lives of others. But when their emotional needs become strong enough, they will ruthlessly and cruelly, though surreptitiously, pursue their own egocentric ends without regard for how they may be hurting others.

Whereas the simple, uncomplicated oppositional child and the chronic underachiever, after they are out from under the domination of their parents, sooner or later break through their patterns of self-defeating oppositionalism, the instrumentally immature child seldom does so. The devices he uses are too resilient socially. There are, unfortunately, too many gullible people in this world who are blind to the mechanisms involved, and there are also too many self-serving but seemingly "kindhearted humanitarians" who, while frequently being indifferent to those who are striving for independence and maturity, will go to great lengths to respond positively to the kinds of inadequacies the instrumentally immature are so skilled in manifesting.

When the instrumentally immature themselves become weary of being the type of persons they are, and make sincere efforts toward self-reliance, it is often too easy to slip out from under their anxieties by appealing to such people for help.

There are, of course, children who are really emotionally immature, who due to severe psychological trauma have failed to develop psychologically past a certain point or else have regressed back to patterns of infantile thinking and emotionality. And there are the mentally retarded who may never develop normal intelligence and self-sufficiency. But the instrumentally immature are neither of these. They are just good actors, so good in fact, that they not only fool their parents and teachers but even themselves.

Like all oppositional children, they are unconscious of what they are doing and, as a result, are the victims of their own actions. Like other oppositional children, they are anxious, depressed, frustrated and secretly hostile; they fear loss of love and feel alienated; they are afraid to risk failure and suffer from intense feelings of inferiority with secret paradoxical ideas concerning their own superiority.

Clinically they show oppositional disturbances in motor-perceptual tasks, blended of course with exaggeratedly immature awkwardness. They drop things and break them, forget and lose things, and generally ruin anything they attempt to do or anything others attempt to get them to do. They seem to be trying so hard to please and are so pathetically apologetic for their shortcomings that one feels extremely heartless when he loses his temper with them.

Instrumentally immature children differ from simple uncomplicated oppositional children in that what they demolish usually belongs to somebody else. As children and as adults, the instrumentally immature are usually careful to avoid hurting themselves. But in both, of course, the ultimate goal is to excite others to rage while remaining themselves tolerant and blameless.

Just as the simple uncomplicated oppositional child is often described as "lazy" by those who feel they really know him, the instrumentally immature child is frequently said to be "selfish." It is remarkable how satisfied parents can be when they hit onto these kinds of explanations for why their children behave they way they do. The truth is that "laziness" and "selfishness" are almost meaningless terms, and to the extent they have any meaning can be applied to all people equally.

The instrumentally immature child is no more selfish

than the simple uncomplicated oppositional child is lazy. They are both desperate. And what is dismissed as "selfishness" in the instrumentally immature is simply a degree of desperation so great that all long-range goals are ruled out, and the child is absolutely dependent emotionally on short-range, immediate gratifications.

He is so hungry for love, so sure that he can never get it, that he is literally greedy for even the most meager indications of sympathy. He has such a low opinion of himself that he feels that only by fraudulent means, by manipulating and forcing others, can he gain even the semblance of acceptance.

And we explain this by saying the child is selfish!

The instrumentally immature child is usually rejected by his peers. Even when he is always smiling and pleasant, always wearing a sweet and angelic expression, he sooner or later exhausts the patience of his friends. No matter how agreeable or self-sacrificing he is, the time comes when he is tolerated only by people who take perverse delight in nurturing the inadequacies of others. No one can really like him. He takes the fun out of any social or work activity. Concessions must be made for him and someone must take the time to talk to him, reassure him, and quell his seemingly endless anxieties. He complains that others don't want him along, and it is true, for most children and adults grow tired of the chore of being nursemaid to a cringing, complaining cry-baby.

In school he falls easily into well-worn ruts. Mrs. Jones is told that the school recommends that her little boy remain another year in kindergarten for he doesn't seem mature enough for the first grade. And Mrs. Jones agrees, for she knows quite well what they are talking about. Her child needs special attention, she is told, and more readiness activities. But in a year, he does not seem a bit better and, if anything, worse, and now he is going into the first grade, a big oversized misfit whom the smaller children will work circles around.

In getting out from under parental pressures, the instrumentally immature child undoes himself by his cleverness. The adults in his environment are usually completely taken in by the masquerade. His mother, who undoubtedly finds his behavior extremely vexing, who may or may not see him as selfish, cruel, and sneaky, views him nevertheless as completely unable to manage his own affairs. He is the cross she must bear, and she never realizes that she unwittingly maintains his immature patterns of behavior.

Brave or foolhardy indeed is the father or teacher who attempts to break up these patterns by insisting on mature behavior, for the instrumentally immature child, when his inadequacies are discounted, possesses an imposing arsenal of heart-rending reactions, from trembling and sobbing all the way through twitching jerks and feigned illness.

Children, on the other hand, are more aware of what the instrumentally immature child is doing. When adults are not around, he is ordinarily treated with jeering contempt by his siblings, playmates, and classmates. With his already impaired capacity for forming mature reciprocal friendships, he learns to dread being left alone with his peers and turns even more resolutely to his parents and other adults for protection. It is interesting that children who are in fact immature intellectually or emotionally, who are really overwhelmed by the ordinary demands of daily living, are not treated this way by their peer group, but on the contrary are usually carefully protected and looked out for.

The instrumentally immature are undoubtedly bright. They would, of course, have to be in order to carry out such convincing performances. It must be emphasized, however, that they are taken in by their performances as is everyone else.

Although at times they may be aware of how they exaggerate their immaturities and secretly harbor paradoxical feelings of superiority, they believe fully as much as everyone around them that they cannot function on their own as well as other children their age. It is heartwarming to observe the buoyant pride of such children when circumstances force them to succeed in a situation where they have had to solve problems completely on their own. A father once related how he goaded his instrumentally immature daughter into realizing that she could tell time. She was a very bright second grader and had been able to correctly interpret the hands on a clock before she was in the first grade, but as part of her pattern of feigned incompetency had seemingly lost this skill. The mother watched in abject horror while the father questioned the child mercilessly.

The situation, as the father described it, had developed casually one evening when, while reading the newspaper, he had asked his daughter to look at the clock and tell him the time. She had come back in a little while with a sad expression on her face and announced that she could not tell. When the father went himself and saw that it was exactly eight o'clock, he became indignant. The child, of course, beautifully displayed her repertoire of sympathy-obtaining reactions. The father sat her down and placed the clock in front of her, and while her sisters and brothers watched in stunned silence, he forcefully ordered her to tell him what time it was. When she whimpered that she did not know, he pulled her up and spanked her, then sat her down and asked her again for the time.

In the brief moment required for this sequence of events, the wife and daughter merged together in a united front against the father, while the rest of the children attempted as best they could to remain neutral. The climax came when the father, ignoring the mother, turned sternly on his daughter and told her in no uncertain terms that he knew that she knew what time it was. Then he asked again, and she said, *"It's eight o'clock."*

The mother blinked her eyes in amazement, and the daughter herself seemed surprised that she was able to give her father the correct answer. The father said, *"That's better!"* and went back to reading the newspaper. The important thing is that the little girl seemed then quite proud of her newly found ability, and when it was time to go to bed, she came and gave her father, who by this time was feeling that he had been something of a heartless ogre, an especially big hug and goodnight kiss.

The point of this story is that the instrumentally immature child does not like to be the way he is. He would rather be competent and self-sufficient as other children are, and he appreciates and respects anyone who compels him to reveal his latent competencies and abilities. And by the same token, were we to follow the life of an instrumentally immature child, we would discover that sooner or later he comes to hate those whom he feels are responsible for allowing him to avoid so easily the challenges and demands of living.

The instrumentally immature child, without realizing it, has sold himself short, and his parents and teachers have acquiesced. He has been allowed, even encouraged, to give up the maturational struggle before it has begun. He has thus been denied his birthright as a human being before he has ever had a chance to find out what that birthright entails. If as an adult he feels cheated, as almost all of the instrumentally immature do, it is certainly not without ample justification.

Clinically, nearly all immature children and adults score low or relatively low on the Comprehension subtests of the Wechslers. The children and adult Wechsler intelligence scales each have a "Comprehension" subtest which is designed to measure what might be called judgment, wisdom, or intellectual maturity.

The questions asked deal with common, everyday matters, and involve differing degrees of understanding. As an item for measuring a child's comprehension, one might ask, *"Why doesn't your mother give you candy every time you ask for it?"* Or one might ask a teenager or adult, *"Why are laws necessary?"* The instrumentally immature, just like those who are really immature intellectually or emotionally, give shallow, low-level answers when asked these kinds of questions.

While the truly immature generally score low on all the subtests of the Wechslers, the instrumentally immature typically score average or above average on the Picture Arrangement subtests. The Picture Arrangement subtests consist of various comic strip pictures presented in a mixed-up order, and it is necessary for the individual being tested to put them into a meaningful order.

It is generally assumed by psychologists that the Picture Arrangement subtests measure "social intelligence," that is, the ability to understand, anticipate and predict other people's behavior. Persons who score low on Comprehension and high on Picture Arrangement, as the instrumentally immature typically do, are very likely to be highly skilled at manipulating others and prone to use this skill to get others to meet their own immature needs.

In their drawings, the intellectually retarded and the emotionally regressed show pervasive inadequacy or disturbance. But despite elaborate efforts at camouflage, the drawings of the instrumentally immature reveal signs of competencies and mature intellect. Their drawings may show distortions and frequent erasures, the human figures may be extremely small, tilted or scrawled across the page, but the hands, for example, will each have five fingers, or other details will be accurately delineated which belie the immaturity of the drawer.

The instrumentally immature, like all oppositional children, commonly draw the human figure with a square body, and like chronic underachievers, often supply this figure with a head which is exaggeratedly flat. Form-perception disturbances due to strong oppositional tendencies, lack of confidence, and constriction of visual field resulting from anxiety are found in the instrumentally immature as in all oppositional children.

But children who are faking their immaturities repeatedly let responses slip through which clearly indicate the latent maturities present. For the astute psychologist, the drawings of the instrumentally immature offer convincing evidence of the mechanisms operating. The Rorschach ink blot responses of the instrumentally immature are very similar to those of other oppositional children, but are distinctly different from the intellectually retarded and the emotionally regressed. Instrumentally immature children frequently make no responses to particular cards or else delay their responses for long periods of time. But they are very rarely able to come up with truly immature responses, and if they do they abandon them quickly if one asks about them.

They may sit during the Rorschach examination with fingers in their mouths, talking with an infantile lisp, but what they relate seeing in the ink blots reveals the concealed hostility, affectional anxiety, and depression of fully developed oppositionalism.

Their Rorschach responses usually show good form, ample motivation, ego-strengths, and creative intelligence. And when tested early enough, at the pre-school and elementary levels, the capacity for forming empathic relationships can still be clearly seen. This is not to say that in the Rorschach protocols of the instrumentally immature, any less than in those of other oppositional children, there is an absence of signs of disturbance.

On the contrary. What the average instrumentally immature child describes in the ink blots would shock most readers: figures with heads cut off, dripping blood, monsters, a person's insides, a cat squashed on the highway, and worse. And all oppositional children frequently give these kind of responses. But interspersed among these kinds of responses are other healthier ones, balancing them, and clearly indicating to the psychologist the capacity that is present for mature, creative adjustment.

Once down the road toward instrumental immaturity, the process, however, is seldom reversed. This is not at all due to the fact that the condition is itself intractable. Patterns of instrumental immaturity are easily changed, as they were changed for Shirley R., the illustrative case at the end of this chapter.

All that has to happen is that the child cease getting rewards for his immature behavior while at the same time getting rewards when he acts a little more mature than he ordinarily does. While the child is still in elementary school, or better yet before, if the significant adults in his life emphatically approve of his perhaps at first feeble attempts to behave and think more maturely, and ignore his immaturities, the instrumentally immature child will soon begin playing and working like any ordinary child.

And when the instrumentally immature child begins to abandon his feigned and exaggerated immaturities, he may reveal real sensitivities and gentleness which can be the basis of developing a new and unusually desirable personality. A child or adult who has delayed success in overcoming his own dependencies and feelings of inadequacy is often good at working with children, the handicapped and the aged. Self-sufficient and capable now of mature reciprocal relationships with others, his needs for love and acceptance strengthen his concern for others, and any lingering signs of immaturity only provide an element of child-like innocence and spontaneity, hardly traits anyone could object to. But the instrumentally immature child is far too often not provided with the kinds of experiences and training that will help him break out of his rut. Oh, there are plenty of people, from his parents on down, who will grumble and complain, and harass him about his immaturities. In fact, the complaining is one reason he becomes increasingly desperate for love and appreciation. But few will dare expect mature behavior from him. And if despite this, he happens on occasion to try to be a little more independent or self-sufficient, rare are the rewards he will get for his efforts.

It seems that our ethical beliefs about how children should be treated, the image we have of the perfect parent and teacher, and the whole idealized concept we have of family and social living are geared to keeping the instrumentally immature child hopelessly trapped.

Middle children are much more likely to develop patterns of instrumental immaturity than are oldest and youngest children. Girls, apparently, are even more vulnerable in this respect than boys. Parents with the best of intentions, even with pride or at least with the belief that they are fulfilling to the utmost their parental obligations, unwittingly reinforce immature behavior most often in their middle children and in their daughters.

The oldest boy carries the groceries and mows the lawn. The youngest is carted out in order to act cute for friends and relatives. The middle child, especially if she is a little girl, remains an "ugly duckling" who is allowed to stand shyly in the corner with her fingers in her mouth, and is only recognized if she breaks something, gets sick, or tries to crawl into her mother's lap.

If she offers to help, she is shooed away. If she tries to act cute, it falls flat. Her anxieties and struggles at school are ignored; that is, until that fateful day when she brings home a note saying she is in danger of failing. Then suddenly she is transported to the center of the family stage, where, if she can possibly help it, she will never leave. She thus finds in her personal failures the secret to perpetual stardom. And despite all the turmoil she will suffer throughout her life because of them, she will never, never give them up, for they will very likely remain the only reliable means that she ever has for filling space in the world of those she loves.

How easy it would be, one thinks, to take some of the time one spends preoccupied with the failings and weaknesses of instrumentally immature children, and devote that time to discovering and applauding their strengths. How much better it would be to nurture their budding attempts to stand on their own feet, to share with them their pride in small achievements, and to have faith in them when they set out to tackle the world on their own. How easy it would be, how much better it would be, and how much more "ideal" should we consider the parent or teacher who attempts to do these things.

Instrumental immaturity in childhood prevents children from developing the maturational skills they must have in order to be successful adults. As parents and teachers we should strive to alter this pattern when it occurs in children before it becomes entrenched and stabilized.

Of all forms of oppositionalism, instrumental immaturity is apparently the most self-defeating and the most alienating, and it is the most difficult for the person himself to overcome. With a little of the right kind of help, children never need to be instrumentally immature. It would certainly be time well spent for each of us to understand what we can about this seemingly needless problem, and do all we can to prevent its occurrence.

Although the clinical signs of instrumental immaturity are more easily discernible than those of other patterns of oppositionalism, the causative factors seem more complicated and difficult to explain. Why, we ask ourselves, does this form of oppositionalism occur, rather than some other form? As a partial answer to this question, it should be pointed out that instrumental immaturity rarely occurs unless there has first been a vulnerability set up in the child.

There are in all children powerful biological and social forces which move them toward maturity, and these have to have been to some degree arrested in order for children to tolerate the emotional and psychological limits immaturity imposes. Furthermore, the kinds of pressures applied by the parents of instrumentally immature children seem much more subtle and much more complex than those applied by the parents of other types of oppositional children, and are usually the result of some kinds of stress the parents themselves are under.

Parents of the instrumentally immature frequently need professional help in overcoming some personal problems of their own. Whereas the parents of simple, uncomplicated oppositional children usually strive for perfection in their children in a straight-forward, unequivocal way, the parents of the instrumentally immature are more uncertain about their goals, and more unsure of how to reach them.

It is interesting in this respect that when pressuring parents begin, for any reason, to doubt the certainty of their convictions, their children tend to manifest seemingly regressive characteristics. When this happens, parents should not be alarmed, but should simply guide them toward increased maturity by ignoring their immaturities and emphatically responding whenever their children attempt greater maturity or independence.

Illustrative Case
Shirley R.

Shirley R. is the youngest of three children. She has two older brothers who seem to be progressing satisfactorily in school. Her mother and father are high school graduates. Her father owns a neighborhood grocery. Shirley did very poor work in the first grade and was required to repeat it.

When first informed that Shirley was doing failing work, her mother had her seen by a psychologist. Mrs. R. told the psychologist that she had felt all along that Shirley was not ready for school, that she was not as alert as other children her age and did not seem to grasp situations as quickly. She said that Shirley's speech was retarded, that she always spoke "baby talk" at home.

She supposed that Shirley's difficulties in learning to read were due, at least in part, to her speech problems. She said that she had to dress Shirley, tie her shoestrings, and do other things for her; that she frequently had trouble getting Shirley to eat properly, and that Shirley had started wetting the bed the previous summer.

Shirley, she said, was shy about making friends, and preferred to be with her, the mother, or to play with paper dolls or color coloring books alone. Mrs. R. said that if it had not been for her husband's insistence, she would have kept Shirley out of school for another year.

The psychologist whom Mrs. R. saw at that time confirmed her fears about Shirley. Shirley, he told her, was found when tested to be functioning intellectually within the "borderline defective" range, about a year and a half behind her chronological age, with a full scale IQ of 74 on the children's Wechsler. The psychologist pointed out to the mother that it might be difficult for her to accept the fact that Shirley is of "subnormal intelligence," but that it was better not to expect too much of the child. The psychologist explained, however, that much of Shirley's difficulties were apparently due to the fact that she was being overprotected and that her attempts to become more mature were frustrated, especially by the mother.

It was recommended that the mother encourage Shirley to be more independent, let her do more things on her own, and not to do so many things for her. Most of all the mother was advised not to correct her so much and not to push her to learn.

Almost two years later, after Shirley has finally been promoted to the second grade, she is referred to the psychological clinic for a second psychological evaluation. She is now nearly 8 years old.

During interviews with the social worker, while Shirley is being tested by the psychologist, the mother reports that Shirley still has the same problems which prompted having Shirley seen by a psychologist two years earlier.

The father, who is present this time, says that he just cannot agree with what the previous psychologist found. Mr. R. believes, for example, that Shirley's speech problems are simply the result of her being overindulged by everyone in the family. For himself, he says, when she does not speak clearly he tells her he does not understand and for her to talk to him again when she can speak more clearly. She is quite capable of speaking clearly, he says, when she is forced to in this way. Furthermore, he states that he is sure that Shirley is quite capable of tying her shoestrings, dressing herself, and eating properly.

His wife, he says, is not consistent with Shirley. On one hand she fusses at Shirley for not being more self-sufficient, then turns around and waits on her "hand and foot." For example, mealtime for Shirley is like she was eating in a restaurant; if Shirley does not like what is being served, Mrs. R. will leave the table and prepare something else for her.

Although he does not approve of her management of Shirley, Mr. R. says that he does not intercede. Mr. R.

Figure 11. *Shirley R.'s Draw-A-Person.*

believes that Shirley will grow out of her speech problems, and that in the meantime, too much pressure applied or too much attention paid to them will only accentuate these problems. He knows that his wife worries too much about Shirley.

The evaluation by the present psychologist is as follows:

> On the Wechsler Intelligence Scale for Children, Shirley demonstrated a Verbal IQ of 87, a Performance IQ of 92, and a Full Scale IQ of 88. She was cautious, anxious, uncertain and could not be rushed. She concentrated very diligently on the test, squirmed in her chair uncomfortably as the tasks became difficult, but was cooperative throughout, smiling easily and attractively when unable to answer. (Author's note:

She scored higher on Digits Backward than Digits Forward.) A qualitative analysis of her test behavior indicates normal intelligence, but her cautiousness in responding lowers her ability to demonstrate this.

She shows exceptionally high social intelligence with some behavioral immaturities, indicating that she is probably highly skilled at manipulating adults. She functions best in a calm, reassuring situation.

On the Wide Range Achievement Test, Shirley demonstrated a Reading Grade of 1.7 and an Arithmetic Grade of 2.3. It is evident that she is uncertain of her ability, and can probably demonstrate greater academic skills in a familiar, calm situation. Stress probably severely curtails her ability to read and do arithmetic.

Her drawings indicate frustration and feelings of inadequacy. But the Rorschach reveals a good feminine identification and basically sound ego-strengths. Relationships between mother and child appear very good at the present time. On none of the tests were there any indications of brain dysfunctions.

Conclusion: Superficial immaturities, anxieties and uncertainties in a child of normal intelligence. No true pathology was found. Parents need to be given accurate information concerning the child's intelligence and encouraged to continue their efforts to allow her to learn more mature patterns of behavior. Shirley has improved markedly since the previous testing, and at the present time it appears that she will continue to improve.

The results of the present evaluation were discussed with the parents. The psychologist stated that he felt that the previous psychologist had been taken in somewhat by Shirley's skill in acting immaturely.

It is certain, he said, that there is nothing wrong with

Shirley's intelligence, and that he tended to agree with Mr. R., namely, that Mrs. R. was being overindulgent and not allowing Shirley to learn to be self-sufficient and independent. Mr. R. was encouraged to take a more active part in child-rearing and to talk more with his wife about any problems she might be having. Mr. and Mrs. R. were strongly advised not to push Shirley, nor criticize or nag her, but to give her opportunity to be more responsible for herself. They should notice and comment favorably when she shows any improvements at all, no matter how small. In other words, the parents were told, emphasize what she does well and not what she does badly.

The psychologist remarked that he had, incidentally, noticed no particular speech problems while testing Shirley, and the mother admitted that the teachers reported that Shirley's speech problems were not as evident at school. The significance of this was discussed.

The parents seemed to understand quite well the causes of Shirley's problems, and seemed greatly relieved that there were positive things that they could do to help her overcome them. The parents were told that the public health nurse would visit them periodically to help with any problems they might have, and that they were welcome to return to the clinic whenever they felt the need.

Subsequent reports from the public health nurse were consistently encouraging. The final report, five years later, is as follows: *"With father's help, the mother has become a great deal less overprotective and pressuring; Shirley is now a very mature little girl; she has just passed to the seventh grade; an average student; no problems."*

CHAPTER 7

Patterns of Superficial Regression: The Pseudo-Mature

Patterns of superficial regression may be present in children who otherwise appear extremely sophisticated and adult-like in speech and mannerisms. Such children typically show little apparent interest in ordinary childhood activities and seem to prefer the company of adults to that of other children. They may, in fact, be given "adult responsibilities," such as minding their younger brothers and sisters, answering the phone, or doing other special little services for their parents.

But what they do is all too often done in a ritualistic, compulsive way with little comprehension. They may make cute, surprisingly mature remarks which are usually those they have heard adults say and which they do not really understand. Their orientation is toward adults, and although at times they may openly show hostility, their pleasures are only the vicarious ones experienced when they achieve some kind of status in the grown-ups' world.

They may do well in school, even exceedingly well, but they function more by rote-memorization than by creative intelligence. When they do not do well they are seen in the psychological clinic, depressed, aloof, confused, but extremely well-mannered.

The pseudo-mature are more often the children of older parents. They are more likely to be the oldest child, or an only child, and to be girls. If they have older brothers or sisters, there is usually a marked age difference between them and the other siblings. They are ordinarily reared by their mothers, with their fathers otherwise preoccupied.

Clinically they are almost indistinguishable from the instrumentally immature. They score relatively low on the Comprehension subtest of the Wechslers, indicating poor judgment, and high on Picture Arrangement, indicating skill in manipulating others. But unlike the instrumentally immature, they may score relatively high on Information, reflecting the effects of intense parental drill and coaching. They suffer from depression and concealed hostility, and are unable to form mature, reciprocal friendships within their peer group.

Like the instrumentally immature, they show all the characteristics of oppositionalism with especially pronounced feelings of alienation, with intense feelings of inferiority, and with paradoxical superiority feelings.

What is most striking about the pseudo-mature is how they combine superficial maturities with superficial immaturities in seemingly contradictory ways. Like the instrumentally immature they can act exceedingly "babyish" when the need arises, but usually they affect a mature demeanor retreating into immaturities only when they feel especially threatened or ill-at-ease.

They are unable, however, to function on their own. Their parents, particularly their mothers, have trained them away from self-sufficiency. They have been taught to think of themselves as a member of some sort of privileged elite who need not be bothered with mundane responsibilities of individual survival.

They must be coaxed, pampered and bribed, even to eat, and they extract full reparations whenever they must be inconvenienced by the failings or oversights of others. As they reach young adulthood their increasingly unreasonable demands make it impossible for them to get along with their parents, and serious rifts occur which thrust them out onto the community.

When forced to face the world on their own, even the demands of ordinary living overwhelm them. They must quickly find someone who will watch over them and save them from the consequences of their immaturities, but who at the same time will also allow them to play a mature, domineering role. For the rich, beautiful or talented there are frequently those who at least temporarily are willing to do these things. But the pseudo-mature with nothing more to offer than magnified conceits may find society rather harsh and indifferent.

Pseudo-maturity is basically an unstable pattern. While the instrumentally immature drift through life simply dependent on others, either staying with their parents or else finding surrogate parents in their friends or mates, the pseudo-mature have a more difficult task.

The trouble is that the pseudo-mature take on many of the unpleasant, domineering traits of their parents, and eventually even the parents themselves find this intolerable. Their bossy, impatient, and smart aleck antics are neither appreciated by their peers nor acceptable to society.

Some learn to curb their impulses, at least in public, but since they do not know how to behave in a way that will bring them the social acceptance they want, they frequently become exaggeratedly withdrawn and shy. They may complain bitterly that people lack the ability to see their unusual talents, but the truth is that unbeknownst to them, people usually accord them more than their rightful share of esteem.

With behind-the-scenes support from all-suffering husbands or wives, who will bolster their egos and cover up for their inadequacies in the same ways their parents did when they were children, the pseudo-mature as adults may learn to make excellent impressions on others. With ample external support they commonly "talk a good line." But their vacillating between roles gets them into positions of authority and responsibility they cannot handle.

They become irresolute at critical moments, defeat themselves by their indecisiveness, and seethe with anger at their own self-imposed frustrations. They even compete with their own children, resenting their achievements while demanding perfection from them, and thus causing them in turn to become chronic underachievers. Worst of all they may disrupt everything, even to driving away friends and relatives by outbursts of rage. The fact that there are always new people who can be taken in by appearances keeps them going for awhile, but sooner or later even the pseudo-mature themselves weary of these charades.

The pseudo-mature consciously strive to control others. In this respect, as in other ways, they are like the instrumentally immature. Both groups believe that if they could just get others to do what they want them to do, all their problems would be solved.

The simple, uncomplicated oppositional and chronic underachievers, on the other hand, despite the fact that their patterns of behavior are obviously retaliative reactions to parental pressures, are much more prone to view their problems as primarily due to some sort of serious failings or weaknesses in themselves. This fact probably accounts at least in part for why these forms of oppositionalism are prone to "spontaneously" disappear with the waning of parental influences (but reappearing, it should be noted, seemingly inexplicably during periods of stress).

Having no reason nor inclination to look inwardly for the sources of their frustrations, the pseudo-mature and instrumentally immature blame others for their unhappiness and thus see their task as one of changing the attitudes and behavior of those around them.

The instrumentally immature, however, do this in a surreptitious manner careful not to disrupt the dependency relationships they need, while the pseudo-mature openly and aggressively attempt to bully people into line, thus playing havoc with their needed dependency relationships. In most cases the pseudo-mature never find a comfortable niche for themselves and must sooner or later face the fact that people in general are not going to accept them the way they are.

Because what they are striving to achieve is basically

contradictory, the pseudo-mature commonly develop more serious psychological disturbances. While struggling with irresolvable conflicts, they fail to seek or discover long-range emotional satisfactions. With insatiable desires for independence, status and patronage, but unable to assume responsibilities, relate to others in a mature manner or to demonstrate real achievement, the pseudo-mature face endless dilemmas.

Even when they successfully hide their inadequacies from the majority of people who know or work with them, there nevertheless grows within them an ever increasing dissatisfaction. Their pattern of self-doubts becomes more clearly neurotic, and they may turn to alcohol, drugs or even suicide. Not infrequently they seek psychotherapy, which if undertaken because of real needs to find new self-concepts and patterns of behavior, may lead to significant improvement. But most persons burdened from childhood with patterns of pseudo-maturity probably struggle along on their own, eventually reaching some sort of maturity, but bitter because of the wasted years and the feeling that others have not appreciated them nor understood their struggles.

What causes children to develop patterns of pseudo-maturity? The answer is of course the same as that for other forms of oppositionalism, namely, relentless though often subtle parental pressures. As we have seen before, however, parental pressures may be reacted to in a variety of ways.

Pseudo-maturity becomes the dominant response pattern when self-directed activities in children are curtailed and only superficial conformity is reinforced. Parents who keep tight controls on all that their children do, who disapprove of tendencies toward independence, and who are accepting of behavior only when it meets their needs as parents, can be reasonably certain that whatever maturity their children achieve will be superficial.

It is not certain, however, that these conditions alone will produce a clear pattern of pseudo-maturity. It is more likely that children will ease out from under these kinds of parental pressures by becoming instrumentally immature. For this reason it is usually only an older mother that has a pseudo-mature child.

In order to produce pseudo-maturity in a child, the mother must have a certain amount of confidence in herself, not be distraught by too many personal problems, and have plenty of time to give ample supervision to the child's activities. She must make decisions for the child in all minor and major areas. In all the little daily chores of life it must be made absolutely clear to the child that "Mother knows best."

The overpowering pressure is relaxed and recognitions are given only when the child behaves exactly the way he is told to behave. The mother of a pseudo-mature child will usually tolerate outbursts of anger, as long as they take place in the privacy of the home, and she is always secretly pleased by the child's many inadequacies and dependencies on her.

But parents who feel justifiably proud of their own competencies and judgment undoubtedly do not really want their children to be inadequate and dependent. All parents certainly hope that their children will grow to be self-sufficient and mature. Some may erroneously believe that their example will be enough to assure this, and when they finally begin to realize that their children are lacking the very traits which they themselves possess, value and take pride in, they are disappointed and mystified.

But when and if this happens it is not inexplicable. It is not inexplicable, that is, unless one harbors the extremely erroneous notion that traits which are not allowed to develop in childhood will somehow or other blossom forth miraculously when children become adults.

The parents of pseudo-mature children, especially the mothers, ordinarily have the ability and inclination to effectively apply sound child-rearing practices. But what they try to achieve is the wrong thing. They should reflect on the fact that for children to grow in confidence, wisdom, and strength of character, their first efforts in these areas should not be restricted and their first successes should not be belittled or ignored.

By what they encourage and recognize, parents determine which of their children's potentialities will become realities and which will decay and disappear. Real maturities are as easy to teach as pseudo-maturities, and in the long run are worth a great deal more.

Illustrative Case
Georgie C.

Georgie is an only child. He is eight years old and is in the second grade. He was brought to the clinic by his mother who insisted that there was no problem, in fact that Georgie is an "ideal boy." She believes that her son is a great deal more intelligent than is realized by his teachers, and that perhaps she should enroll him in a school more sensitive and challenging to the abilities of superior children.

Mrs. C., a woman in her early forties, is active in civic affairs and politics, having been elected to several positions in the city government. Her husband is a meteorologist. They both have Master's degrees. Georgie is their only child. During the testing he acted quite mature, and he seemed to enjoy the testing and appeared to be doing his best.

The conclusions of the following report were discussed with the mother, who apparently rejected them. She did not argue with the findings, but simply smiled patronizingly. Mrs. C. never contacted the clinic again, and there is no follow-up information available on Georgie.

On the Wechsler Intelligence Scale for Children, Georgie demonstrated a Verbal IQ of 90, a Performance IQ of 106, and a Full Scale IQ of 97. He scored below average on Comprehension and Digit Span, and scored very low on Similarities and Block Design. He scored above average on Information, Picture Completion, Picture Arrangement and Coding.

It appears that his general intellectual ability is

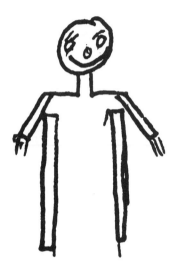

Figure 12. *Georgie C.'s Draw-A-Person.*

above average, but anxiety and compulsivity lower his immediate recall, reasoning, judgment and general usable intelligence. He has, however, a good fund of general information. He is emotionally immature, is apparently skilled at manipulating others, and uses this skill in order to get his immature needs met.

The Rorschach indicates difficulties in making a masculine identification, and pervasive problems in relating to others. He shows deep anxiety, depression and hostility concerning his peers, parents and himself. His relations with his mother seem particularly disturbed. His Draw-A-Person suggests that he feels pressured to achieve more socially and academically than he comfortably can.

On the Wide Range Achievement Test, he demonstrated reading at the 2.6 grade level and arithmetic at the 2.1 grade level. He is in the second grade.

Conclusions: Georgie's parents place too much emphasis on social conformity. Georgie has not been allowed nor encouraged to develop independence and maturity of judgment. He feels pressured by his parents, especially by his mother, and expends much of his mental energies in controlling the resultant hostility. For this reason he is not able to function intellectually at the level he should. He probably has above-average innate intelligence, but is functioning below average verbally.

The parents should strive to give Georgie more freedom and more opportunities to just enjoy himself. They should continue to be interested in what he achieves, but should not continually strive for perfection. They need to learn to take a more relaxed, tolerant attitude toward his social conduct and let him become more independent and self-sufficient.

CHAPTER 8

Patterns of Superficial Regression: Transient Autistic Reactions

By acting hopelessly inadequate and inept, children can usually extinguish their parents' tendencies to pressure them. Parents are very likely to abandon coercion when they are convinced that their children are simply unable to do any better. For this reason, instrumentally immature children learn to avoid mature behavior and resort to babyish tearfulness and tantrums when faced with any ordinary parental demands. These devices, however, do not always work.

Sometimes children who have been allowed or even encouraged to be grossly immature are suddenly subjected to new and unreasonable parental pressures. They find themselves being harassed and criticized relentlessly for behavior which previously had gained them special considerations and concessions.

Marked changes in the way parents treat children can occur because circumstances may abruptly switch parental sympathies away from the children and onto themselves. One of the parents may become seriously ill, physically or mentally, or the parents may find themselves under unusual economic, social or marital pressures. Whatever the reasons, children who have learned to rely primarily on immaturities as a way out of most threatening situations are unprepared for dealing with such crises. With superficial regression as their only adjustment technique, they are caught in an emotional blind alley with no apparent avenues of escape.

Instrumentally immature children subjected to new and harsh parental pressures usually regress even further, becoming more inadequate, immature and, in some instances, extremely withdrawn. Those that withdraw do so not in a gradual way, but rather precipitously and dramatically. Within a matter of days they lose all interest in their environment, and apparently no longer can concentrate on even the simplest tasks and activities.

Their withdrawals closely resemble those of childhood autism, a most serious psychological disorder, and for this reason are called transient autistic reactions. But unlike true autistic withdrawal, the autistic-like reactions of pressured children are nearly always relatively temporary, terminating after a few weeks or months when parental pressures are relieved.

The fact that these transient autistic reactions are typically short-lived, however, does not mean that the underlying maladjustment changes. Children characteristically recover from these intense, short-term withdrawal episodes only to take up again their well-established patterns of instrumental immaturity.

In the clinic, it is not always easy to distinguish transient autistic reactions of pressured children from true autism. Seemingly detached from reality, oblivious to their surroundings and indifferent to everything being done for them or to them, the transiently autistic, no less than the truly autistic, may sit as if somnambulistic, passively gazing out a window or toward a blank wall, while their worried parents intensely discuss their strange behavior.

Parents under such circumstances are ordinarily loath to suggest things which may have contributed to their children's psychological condition, and thus from what can be observed and from what is related there may be little at first on which to base a differential diagnosis. But on psychological tests, the behavior of children whose autistic-like reactions are transitory and due to excessive parental pressures is quite different from that of more seriously disturbed autistic children.

In general, the more disturbed children are emotionally, the more difficult they are to test. The transiently autistic, therefore, while being very difficult to test, are much less so than the truly autistic of whom it can be said are typically impossible to test. Most significant is the fact that during a single testing session the transiently autistic may little by little become more responsive, revealing an immediate capacity for recovery rarely discernible in authentic cases of childhood autism.

In the initial stages of psychological testing the transiently autistic may be uncommunicative, but in a relaxed and supportive atmosphere their defensiveness melts somewhat, and they respond at least to those questions which can be answered briefly or with a nod or shake of the head.

As they begin to talk more freely their speech may be halting, expressionless and without animation, and throughout the testing they may continue to act as if ordinary conversation required enormous amounts of effort. But as testing continues they give more and more scoreable responses. Their typical delays in responding, which at the outset are sometimes so great that they seem to forget what was asked or how they intend to answer, become noticeably shorter, and toward the end, answers may even be volunteered to questions left unanswered earlier.

One should not conclude, however, that these gradual improvements in test-taking are ever enough for valid IQ's to be obtained. In terms of their true levels of ability, the transiently autistic always score low on tests of intelligence, some very low indeed.

Obvious signs of oppositionalism observed in the behavior and test protocols of severely withdrawn and apathetic children serve as convincing diagnostic proof that the reactions in these cases are more or less temporary ones due to sudden and excessive parental pressures. The transiently autistic, on psychological tests, perform as typical oppositional children of the instrumentally immature type.

On the Wechsler Intelligence Scale for Children, they score relatively low on Comprehension and relatively high on Picture Arrangements. Figure-ground reversals and other motor-perceptual disturbances indicative of oppositionalism are seen in their Wechsler Block Designs, Rorschachs, and Bender-Gestalts. Evidence of oppositional traits in children reassures us that they have not yet given up the psychological struggle, and are, perhaps unconsciously, still attempting to resist parental domination.

Oppositional traits are always indicative of inner psychological strength. As has been emphasized before, they occur only in children with well-developed needs and capacities for empathic attachments. Oppositionalism is the only way many empathic children can remain involved with their parents and yet defend themselves from ego-damaging parental attacks.

While oppositional children usually feel alienated they are not in fact alienated. Children who really are alienated are far less sensitive to their parents' disapprovals, and have little inclination to expend their time and energies in fruitless stalemates with them. In authentic cases of childhood autism, for example, oppositional traits are usually absent; when they are present, which is rare, they always represent unusual emotional assets which materially enhance the chances that these otherwise seriously disturbed children will respond favorably to psychiatric treatment.

Most apathetic, disinterested and unresponsive children are not seriously disturbed, but are reacting in an autistic way because of their inability to cope constructively with parental pressures. They are temporarily suspended emotionally, waiting for things to get better. Capable of responding in a normal manner, they simply have lost all reasons to do so. Transient autistic reactions are for them the last stage of a long series of unsuccessful attempts to gain some control over their own lives.

Yet they still love and admire their parents, and the inner rage they feel overwhelms them with guilt, depression and anxiety. Whatever they do falls short of gaining unqualified parental approval.

Because they feel lost and helpless without their parents' support, having no confidence in themselves because of their parents' obvious lack of confidence in them, they are afraid to retaliate or strike out on their own. Thus they are driven into instrumental immaturity in desperate measure to evade this dilemma, and when they find that parental pressures continue unabated or are even increased, withdrawing into fantasy is their only remaining alternative.

Transient autistic reactions, like true autism, are highly motivated attempts to lose contact with reality. They fall short of this disastrous goal and the children recover because the emotional ties between parent and child are strong.

The very reasons, paradoxically, that parents relentlessly criticize and harass their children, namely, their love for them and identification with them, are why most children cannot disengage completely from the real world and lose themselves permanently in fantasy. As unrewarding as their lives may be, there are still things such children want to preserve or regain, and given any chance at all will not abandon them.

Most parents are bewildered and even frightened when their children suddenly lose all enthusiasm for living and seem completely lost in intense self-preoccupations. They should be, for such behavior is a definite warning that something very serious is wrong. Parents should first look to what they are doing, and if at all possible seek psychiatric help. It may come as a rude shock to realize that such reactions can be the product of nothing more than well-meaning but overzealous parental disapprovals and punitive restrictions.

Parents, by being relentlessly hypercritical, unnecessarily cut off major sources of pleasure and happiness which children desperately need in order to successfully face the everyday challenges of growing up. Under continual psychological stress and with little that is fun in their lives, children stagnate emotionally and intellectually. They become dumb, blind and indifferent.

Because they are children, they have not as yet developed the more constructive kinds of insulating defenses and escapes which in most cases will become available later in life. Experiences which adults would find only annoying or irritating can be to them almost totally devastating. They need their parents' loyal support and encouragement, and they cannot function effectively when subjected to repeated attacks on their self-confidence.

Transient autistic reactions, like all oppositional behavior, are due to parental pressures. They subside quickly when some pleasures and rewards are introduced into children's lives. When withdrawal episodes occur, heart-to-heart talks and moralizing lectures are of little value. Children seldom know what is wrong or why, and even if they did, could not alter their behavior on their own or explain it to their parents. It remains for the parents to simply use less coercion and allow children to discover on their own the things they like to do.

And most of all, when children begin to recover normal

responsivity and interests, parents should not frustrate or ridicule their efforts toward self-sufficiency and independence. Cooperating with their children's desires to become responsible and mature, even when what they are doing falls short of what one might ultimately consider satisfactory, is the most effective way parents can be sure that their children will overcome patterns of superficial regression.

Ignoring their immaturities and emphatically approving of their attempts to achieve more mature behavior strengthens children's determination and aspiration to become the kind of adults their parents would desire them to be.

Illustrative Case
Carl A.

During the summer before starting the first grade Carl is brought to the clinic because, as his mother says, he seems to be "*afraid of everything*." Carl is six years old, the oldest of three children. He is, Mrs. A. says, extremely timid and shy, and is neither affectionate nor responsive to gestures of friendship.

Sometimes he will start to play with other children, but somehow he never seems to follow through; most of the time all he does is watch other children play. He will sometimes sit and stare at nothing for hours. He is so withdrawn and preoccupied, his mother says that she is concerned that unless something is done he will not be able to adjust to school.

Mrs. A. states that he has not always been this way. Before the birth of the youngest child, he was perhaps somewhat immature and overly dependent for his age, but essentially normal; after the birth his behavior changed and he became as he is now, moody and unresponsive. The birth of the youngest child, the mother explains, created quite a problem for the family. The youngest child was born with a serious physical disability which necessitated long hours of the mother's time, and involved many emotional and economic crises for her and her husband. The mother describes herself as always having been highly nervous, and this problem with the youngest child kept her in an almost continual state of anxiety. As a result, Carl was frequently ignored during this period, and was expected more or less to fend for himself.

At first, he seemed to manage quite well, taking care of himself and helping out with the middle child. She remembers how thankful she was that Carl had become so self-sufficient, mature and independent. He seemed *"older than he was,"* she relates. Then his behavior began to fluctuate. He began to act more immature and helpless. Before the parents had time to realize what had happened, Carl had become as he is now.

When he was told that he was coming to the clinic for testing, Carl said, *"OK, but it won't do any good."*

Figure 13. *Carl A.'s Draw-A-Person (at age 6).*

The psychologist's report is as follows:

On the Wechsler Intelligence Scale for Children, Carl demonstrated a Verbal IQ of 92, a Performance IQ of 93, and a Full Scale IQ of 92. He scored below average on Comprehension (denoting below-average general judgment) and Mazes (denoting below-average ability to control impulsivity and plan ahead), and low on Information (denoting a poor fund of general information) and Coding (denoting a poor ability to maintain sustained attention and concentration on a simple, routine paper-and-pencil task).

On all the other subtests he scored in the average range except for Similarities (ability to abstract verbally), which was a little above average.

Figure 14.
Carl A.'s Bender Designs
(at age 6).

Observation of Carl during the Wechsler testing revealed that he tends usually to have a "dreamy" expression, tends to forget questions asked him, and there seems to be a slight but constant tremor of his hands and a slight babyish lisp when he talks. Qualitative analysis of the Wechsler would suggest potential intelligence above average (IQ of at least 110). Losses are due to emotional problems.

On the Wide Range Achievement Test, Carl demonstrated sight reading at the .5 grade level (mid-kindergarten), and arithmetic at the 1.1 grade level (beginning first grade). It is apparent that his reading readiness is not as fully developed as it should be in terms of his intelligence, but his arithmetic skills are appropriate for his age and intelligence.

His drawings and Rorschach protocol indicate extreme constriction and withdrawal. There is a decidedly autistic flavor to his drawings, but the Rorschach indicates that reality ties are still intact but that there are few rewards for him when he interacts with his environment. It appears that were his environment to become rewarding he would immediately become more responsive and reality oriented. How long his reality ties will remain intact if changes in his environment do not occur cannot be predicted.

Conclusion: Situational factors producing withdrawal and autistic-like behavior in a boy of normal intelligence whose ties with reality and capacity for normal response are intact. Total family counseling is needed, but if this is not possible, therapy for Carl should be instigated.

Discussion with Mr. and Mrs. A. following the psychological evaluation was centered on the fact that Carl's emotional reactions are due to the unusual psychological pressures he was under during the period of crises involving the youngest child. It was explained to the parents that Carl's initial efforts to be more mature and responsible, and to help during this period had gained him nothing. What he did to help was taken for granted, and he was noticed only when he fell short of parental expectations.

All he really needed at the time was for one or both of his parents to remark on what a good job he was doing and to let him know how much they appreciated it. It is understandable (considering the stress the parents were under) that they failed to do this, but be that as it may, not receiving any recognition for his efforts, receiving only criticism for his failings, caused Carl to give up. Under the circumstances he felt lonely, unloved and frustrated.

The psychological evaluation was discussed in detail, and the parents were reassured that there was nothing wrong with Carl's ability. Carl's problems, the parents were told, are completely emotional, and if these emotional problems can be alleviated, his abilities will become increasingly evident.

Mrs. A. seemed more understanding of Carl's emotional reactions and sensitivities than did her husband. Mr. A. seemed inclined to ignore Carl's problems, believing that they would resolve themselves with the passage of time. It is possible, the father was told, that this may be the case. It is possible, even likely, that with the parents no longer completely preoccupied with the youngest child, Carl will revert back to his previously somewhat immature and dependent behavior. But, the father was asked, is this what is desired?

What the parents missed, it was pointed out, was the opportunity provided by the crises with the youngest child to reward and strengthen mature behavior in Carl. To let him revert back now to his previous behavior would be another opportunity missed.

During this rather lengthy discussion, Mr. A. came to understand more and more what he could do to help Carl gain greater maturity and self-confidence, and seemed more and more willing to cooperate with his wife in this undertaking. Mrs. A., on the other hand, seemed to understand the situation from the first, and she volunteered to come periodically to discuss her and Carl's problems with the social worker, and to report on any progress; with this, the father also agreed to come when he could. He insisted, however, that now that they understood how Carl's problems had come about, he and his wife should be able to work toward solving them on their own.

Mrs. A. did come in more or less regularly. She stated that the sessions with the social worker, in addition to helping her in her relationship with Carl, helped her in solving her own personal problems. Mr. A. also came in on occasion, and reported that he was following the advice of the staff. They both reported that Carl had greatly improved.

Two years later, when Carl was eight, and when he was two months into the third grade, he was seen again by the psychologist for a re-evaluation. The report of that re-evaluation is as follows:

> At the present time on the Wechsler Intelligence Scale for Children, Carl demonstrated a Verbal IQ of 101, a Performance IQ of 101, and a Full Scale IQ of 101. Although there is a tendency for him to be satisfied with casual performance on some subtests and this lack of optimal motivation for accuracy lowered some of his subtest scores, his present test behavior shows markedly improved ability to concentrate and plan ahead. No tremor or lisp was observed, and he appeared attentive, alert, and confident. Although his IQ scores are not quantitatively superior to those obtained two years ago, his general functioning seems markedly improved.
>
> On the Wide Range Achievement Test, he

Figure 15. *Carl A.'s Draw-A-Person (at age 8).*

demonstrated reading at the 3.9 grade level and arithmetic at the 3.8 grade level. In view of the fact that he is now in the third grade, it appears that his school achievement is clearly satisfactory.

His drawings still show some feelings of uncertainty and some lack of confidence, but show marked improvement and no evidence of emotional constriction. He is perhaps somewhat immature, but seems to be developing in a mature direction.

The present Rorschach reveals improved ability to relate to his peers, but this ability is still impeded and not fully developed. He has formed a warm, affectionate relationship with his father and is comfortable in the male role. He now views his mother as a stable figure in his life. He feels more comfortable

Figure 16. *Carl A.'s Bender Designs (at age 8).*

in dealing with the world as a whole. But his ambition has not developed as it should, and he seems to be maintaining a sort of dependent immaturity. In general, the Rorschach shows marked emotional and social improvement.

Conclusions: Marked social and emotional improvement in a boy of normal intelligence who previously showed rather serious autistic withdrawal. At present he seems, however, somewhat immature, dependent and unambitious, not being concerned enough about accuracy in his work, and as a result has not as yet realized his full intellectual potential. He needs help now in forming relationships with his peers on his own and in developing a mature pattern of independence and sense of responsibility.

Mr. and Mrs. A. were seen for a final interpretive interview. The social worker's report of that interview is as follows:

> Parents were seen for joint interview with the psychologist and social worker at which time previous findings were compared to present test results. Recognition was given to help received from parental counseling. Initial emphasis was placed on the rather marked global improvement in evidence. Current problems were related not only to progress made but to further help needed.
>
> It was pointed out that Carl is somewhat immature but he is developing in a mature direction. Some specific suggestions were offered regarding methodology in helping Carl become more independent, ambitious, and responsible. Inconsistencies in approach to and handling of tasks are evident. Carl either does something perfectly, sloppily or not at all, but he is less fearful and constricted than formerly. Parents readily agreed and gave illustrations in support of their conception of him as really quite a smart and unusual child.
>
> Mrs. A. pointed to continued improvement in academic performance and attributed this to less disturbance in the home, and less arguments between parents. She is no longer plagued with nervousness and severe headaches.
>
> Recognition was given to improved relationship and degree of emotional honesty presently existent between parents as a result of having tackled the problem head-on and taking some appropriate action. Parents are proud of what they have been able to accomplish and confident that they will be able to sustain gains made and provide the kind of help their

son needs.

Reassurance was given around our continued interest and availability for further assistance. Carl seems to be on the right course now, but should he get off, his parents are better equipped to cope effectively with the situation.

His mother alluded to the consultant's previous remark relative to a child being a mirror of a parent's problems. She and her husband have come to fully appreciate the meaning of this statement and found it virtually impossible to explain even to themselves how the improved situation they now enjoy was achieved.

Four years later a follow-up report by the public health nurse was optimistic: *"Carl is going into the seventh grade; he is a good student, and there seem to be no problems; the father is much more understanding, and the mother is much less nervous."*

CHAPTER 9

The Habitually Hostile Child

Children who have habits of behaving in hostile and aggressive ways are almost universally disliked. They are disliked by their peers, siblings, neighbors, teachers, and not infrequently by their parents. Strange as it may seem, children who are habitually hostile and aggressive are so usually because of strong needs to be liked. They are anxious and lonely, and they want people to like them, but they do not know how to achieve this end. Because they are not liked, they feel frustrated and bitter. They see people around them ignoring them and trying to avoid them, and when they have taken all the indifference and rejection from others that they can, they lash out at them. There may not be much sense in the direction their rage may take, and they may attack those whom they have least reason to resent. And after venting their rage they feel even more anxious and alone, even more rejected and frustrated, and even more likely to lash out again.

The habitually hostile child learns early that his behavior is not going to earn him the love and affection he so desperately wants. He knows as well as anyone that being hostile and aggressive drives people away. But he does not know how to behave otherwise. He knows that he is not loved, and what is worse, that he is not lovable. For this reason he cannot trust those who try to befriend him; he knows that no one could honestly want a person like him around. And he is sure that no one will ever want him around. He knows that people will keep him away from them if they possibly can, and he remains in a more or less constant state of anger and anxiety because of this, and because he sees this rejection as permanent and unchangeable.

If the habitually hostile child should from time to time curb his unsociable acting out, and by doing nothing at all for a while gain a little acceptance from his peers and family, he knows that the meager acceptance he will receive will do little toward ridding him of the vast loneliness and frustration he feels. He knows, too, that sooner or later this meager acceptance will become intolerable and he will revert to his customary way of dealing with people.

The suspense of knowing that he cannot control impulsivity for long makes him feel, during any period of suspended activity, as anxious and angry as he would feel if he were acting out at his worst.

This almost intolerable high state of anxiety and anger, from which the habitually hostile child is seldom free, undermines his self-control and drives him to act in socially undesirable ways. His "social intelligence" is usually poor, and he has not learned how to channel nervous energy into socially desirable activities. He has never acquired habits of behaving in such a way as to regularly win friendship and respect.

What he has acquired are habits of causing trouble. Driven by anxiety and anger, he literally seeks out situations in which he can be at his worst. It is as if he must make others pay for his misery. Observing him, one gets the impression that he is constantly searching for a chance to break something, disrupt the activities of others, or hurt someone.

The habitually hostile child is, of course, achieving the exact opposite of what he really wants to achieve. He wants desperately to be loved, and yet he earns everyone's hatred. In his particular style of oppositionalism it is his anger that is most obvious. But behind this anger are all the feelings other oppositional children experience. For example, he is afraid that he is not smart enough, and afraid that only if his parents believe that he is smart will they ever love him. He feels alienated and is miserably unhappy and depressed. And most of all, like all oppositional children, he has no idea of why he is the way he is, nor does he know how to change.

Habitual hostility in a child is not simply the result of parental pressures, but rather is the result of pressure combined with rejection and neglect. The habitually hostile child is ignored until he does something which inconveniences or embarrasses his parents, and then he receives vehement criticism. He is ignored as much as possible, and left to fend for himself.

If he does not create problems for them, his parents live their lives as if he did not exist. If he should try to talk with them or share an experience with them, they become impatient and irritable. They let him know by their actions that they simply do not have time to be bothered with him. And, of course, like the parents of all oppositional children, they never fail to let him know that whatever he does that is good is never good enough, and that no matter what he might achieve, it will never come up to his parents' exalted standards.

Now the parents may have fallen into this kind of relationship with their child out of necessity. Both the mother and the father may be engaged in demanding work that leaves them fatigued and preoccupied when they are away from it. They may be harassed by severe financial or health problems. They may be battling with intense emotional problems which leave them with little time or energy for others. They may have to be away from the child a great deal of the time.

In short, the neglect of the child may not be of the parents' choosing, and their lack of patience with the child may be something they just cannot help. But be that as it may, a child will become habitually hostile only if he is neglected by his parents and is led to believe that they do not really care what happens to him.

While being left to fend for oneself is essential in the causation of habitual hostility in children, it should be remembered that neglect alone is not sufficient. To become habitually hostile, a child must also be subjected to unremitting disapproval and criticism. But is it necessary for parents who neglect a child to also have to constantly disapprove of him and criticize him? Why, if they have so little time to give to the child, do they not use that time in strengthening his self-confidence and in reinforcing his best tendencies?

There are probably many answers to this question, not the least common of which is the parents attempt to blame the child for their own feelings of guilt for neglecting him. But in many cases the parents use the time they have with the child to disapprove of him and criticize him simply because they are ignorant of what is the most effective means of bringing out the best in a child.

The parent may feel that since they have so little contact with the child, they should use what time they do have for identifying as many of his faults and shortcomings as possible, in order to correct them. But the more they criticize the child, the more they have to criticize, for constant criticism will usually achieve the opposite of what parents are trying to achieve by using it.

When the parents feel guilty for the way they neglect their child they may complain to the child of his failings while, in order to assuage their guilt, lavishing gifts on him. Sometimes such parents even arm the child with pellets or BB guns, firecrackers or other dangerous "toys," and turn him loose on a defenseless neighborhood.

It should be emphasized that giving expensive gifts to a child when he has done nothing to earn them does little to reassure a child that his parents accept and love him. And, of course, it is socially and morally reprehensible to give a child dangerous playthings when he has not learned how to use them responsibly.

Children from economically deprived areas and from broken homes, since they are more likely to be neglected, are more likely to be habitually hostile. It should be noted, however, that the vast majority of children from economically deprived areas are not habitually hostile, nor are those from broken homes. And a large number of the habitually hostile children that one sees in schools and in the child guidance clinics are neither from economically deprived areas nor broken homes. It should also be noted that the vast majority of juvenile delinquents are not habitually hostile, nor are the majority of habitually hostile children delinquent; juvenile delinquency is a complex phenomenon with much more complex sociological and psychological causes than habitual hostility.

It is not at all unusual to discover, upon meeting them, that the parents of the notorious little hellion of a neighborhood or school, who has everyone at their wits' end trying to cope with him, are themselves charming, considerate, and college-educated. This fact apparently reflects a serious weakness in what constitutes a liberal education.

It sometimes seems that many of the college-educated learn so many things that they should not do as parents that when they finally become parents they end up doing nothing. Having children because they vaguely feel that they should, or because their mate wants to, or simply because it is the fashion, many young and otherwise refined and well-educated fathers and mothers push their children out the door in the morning and hook the door behind them in the vain hope that by doing so they will be free of the responsibility for them for the day. Sooner or later such parents will pay dearly for this sort of self-indulgence, and at some point in their education they should have been warned of the consequences of this way of handling children.

The habitually hostile child, unlike other types of oppositional children, openly rebels against parental neglect and pressure. Although he shares with other oppositional children a bitterness and unhappiness, due to never receiving recognition for his best efforts but only criticism for his failures, the habitually hostile child spurns the subterfuge other oppositional children so frequently use and sets out to fight back openly. Although he may attack those whom he has least reason to attack, at least his battles are out where everyone can see them.

His parents, who may at first not realize the full range and extent of his destructiveness, eventually will have to face the consequences of it. Either the child will, if he has not done so at the outset, turn his aggression directly onto them, or the parents will be disagreeably appraised of their child's disruptive behavior by neighbors, school officials, or the police.

Because he vents his anger openly, the habitually hostile child cannot be easily ignored. The fact that he makes everyone around him miserable forces others to seek some sort of solution to his problem. Everyone has a vested interest in his becoming better adjusted, more settled, and less hostile. His ever-present destructiveness not only compels his parents to learn more effective ways of dealing with him, but his peers, neighbors and teachers also feel compelled to search for solutions to his problems.

With all the community concern his actions stir up, it should not be surprising that the habitually hostile child has a better chance of finding his way out of the psychological trap he has gotten into than do other types of oppositional children.

What may be more surprising is the fact that many, if not most, habitually hostile children grow up to be rather pleasant and somewhat exaggeratedly considerate adults. Because of their deep yearnings to be accepted and liked, once habitually hostile children hit upon ways of behaving which gain them friendships and respect, they find the rewards enormously gratifying.

Although they may appear somewhat aggressively desperate for friendship, prone to over-react to supposed slights, and too quick in voicing criticisms of others, adults who were habitually hostile as children are often worthwhile people with strong concerns for the welfare of others.

Because they are so late in learning human relationship skills they may never learn them well, but what they may lack in social finesse they often more than make up for by their deep and sincere desire to be liked and respected by others. If one were to interview the most successful and dedicated school counselors, Scoutmasters, teachers and youth workers, he would find that a disproportionately large number report that they themselves were severe discipline problems when they were young. And it is a reflection of the insight that they have into themselves that most of those who were habitually hostile as children are very effective in working with children who are habitually hostile.

Adults who have overcome their own childhood habitual hostility may be very effective in working with habitually hostile children and are very unlikely to neglect their own children as they themselves were neglected, and therefore are hardly the type of persons who as parents would produce habitual hostility in their children. This does not mean that they will not be pressuring parents.

On the contrary, adults who as children were habitually hostile are highly prone to be hard taskmasters, and like parents who were chronic underachievers as children, are often filled with the righteous zeal of being sure that *"their children do not make the same mistakes they made."* Inspired by this kind of zeal, although they may be quite good in working with other people's children, they are unfortunately very likely to create some form of oppositionalism in their own.

Illustrative Case
Terry G.

Terry is six years old and is the oldest of three children. He was referred to the clinic because at school he *"does not submit to authority or follow directions."* He manifests hostility frequently, is extremely restless and has the habit of forcefully and repeatedly bumping his head against his chair or desk during classroom study periods. Terry's parents are both extremely busy professional people; his mother is at the present time working on an advanced degree.

Terry's teacher submitted the following report concerning Terry's behavior in school:

> Terry has been a behavior problem since the first day of school. He has the intelligence to do his work but not the ability to concentrate or to work without constant supervision.
>
> He does not respond to the usual rewards for good school work. Punishments also seem to have no effect on Terry. He seems to like to stay in at recess. He does not respond to paddling. He cries but soon continues the same behavior. Terry does respond to pampering, special jobs, and quiet talks. However, even with this he refuses to work unless I stand over him every minute.
>
> Terry is a most baffling child because he is at the same time mature and immature, loving and unloving, able to work but not willing to work. He is mature in some ways and often seems to have the speech and mannerisms of an adult. He seems himself as an adult in that he thinks he has the right to correct children and *"teach them a lesson."*
>
> Terry is immature in that if he does not get his way he pouts, kicks, slaps, bites, and spits. He refused to go to lunch once because he could not be first in line. He has bitten two children that I know of because he did not have his way. He spit on one child. Very seldom does a recess go by that Terry has not hurt someone. In spite of his behavior the children do not show any great dislike for him.
>
> Terry shows little or no respect for adults. On one occasion when I told him to do a work sheet he told me I could *"stick it up my nose."* Recently when I told him to take out a *Weekly Reader* to read with the class, he took it out and tore it up—not two feet away from me. He is quick to say he is sorry, but also quick to do the

same thing again.

Often he acts like a baby and practically crawls up in my lap. He seems to crave affection and wants it from everyone.

He has shown cruelty to animals. He likes to kill bugs and talks about killing birds with a slingshot. One day he came to school with a jar of live bugs with pins stuck in their backs.

There is a question whether or not Terry should pass to the second grade. He is able to do the work but only with a maximum of supervision. His behavior may become even worse if he has to repeat first grade.

The psychologist's report is as follows:

On the Wechsler Intelligence Scale for Children, Terry demonstrated a Verbal IQ of 97, a Performance IQ of 74 and a Full Scale IQ of 85. He shows a little above average immediate recall. His fund of information, ability to abstract verbally, ability to plan ahead and control impulsivity all test at the average level, but there are inconsistencies in how he functions in these areas.

His judgment and ability to identify logical detail errors are poor. His social intelligence, form perception, and speed at routine paper-and-pencil tasks are very poor. During the testing he frequently rocked back and forth, appeared restless, and was easily distracted. He slouched in his chair and would occasionally breathe out and sigh as if the testing were a great burden.

On the Wide Range Achievement Test, he demonstrated reading at the 1.9 grade level. He demonstrated arithmetic at the 2.3 grade level. Since he is in the first grade, these scores indicate fairly good academic achievement, but he is not consistent in his

Figure 17. *Terry G.'s Draw-A-Person.*

reading and arithmetic skills, and probably cannot reliably demonstrate a knowledge of first grade work. (Incidentally, he is inclined to show mirror reversals in his reading and writing.)

His Draw-A-Person reveals major difficulties with form and also indicates that he feels pressured to achieve more socially and academically than he comfortably can. His Bender drawings show separations and loss of form possibly indicative of minimal brain dysfunction.

The Rorschach shows intact reality ties, but strong tendencies to feel persecuted in any new situation. He feels alienated from the others and in turn is hypercritical of others. He apparently has no insight into himself. He is, however, potentially able to form empathic relations with both adults and other children. He has made a good masculine identification and is comfortable in the masculine role. He is normally ambitious but does not have any idea of how he can realize his ambitions. Except for the feelings of persecution he manifests, his Rorschach shows no serious emotional difficulties, no hostility, uncontrolled impulsivity, depression nor anxiety. Furthermore, there are no signs of brain dysfunction in the Rorschach.

Conclusion: Feelings of persecution and of being pressured in a normally intelligent boy. It is very unlikely that minimal brain dysfunction is present. His restlessness and distractibility seem to be the result of feelings of being persecuted and pressured, and do not seem to be due to uncontrollable impulsivity.

He is oppositionalistic and instrumentally immature, and his academic and social behaviors are very inconsistent. Apparently the relationships between him and his parents are disturbed and inconsistent. It seems clear that this boy will become an increasingly serious conduct problem if improved methods of dealing with him are not discovered and utilized.

During the discussions with Mr. and Mrs. G. concerning Terry's problems, it was explained to them by the staff that it is not just their busy schedule that is having a detrimental effect on Terry's social and educational development, but the fact that when they are with Terry they fail to support and encourage his best efforts.

Feeling neglected, they were told, is only part of the cause of Terry's problems. He also feels rejected and totally disapproved of. Mr. and Mrs. G. were advised to try to look for things that Terry does that could be praised, little things that might be a bit better than what he ordinarily does, and give the praise for these things without bringing up any of his faults. Let him see, they were told, that at least some things he does are right, and let him enjoy for the moment his little successes.

Terry's parents at first seemed to believe that he did little that could be praised. But the more that they talked about it the more worthwhile things they could remember Terry having done, and they seemed to realize how they had habitually failed to emphasize Terry's good qualities to him.

They admitted that they seldom talked to him about anything but his failings or shortcomings, and they saw clearly now, they said, how this must make him feel.

It was emphasized that Mr. and Mrs. G. should not now lavish praise on Terry, nor try to make up to him for past neglect. What they should do is try each day to find something good that Terry has done and comment on it. Terry should not be treated in such a way as to expect only criticism from his parents; when he does something a little better than ordinary, he should expect that his parents will notice and remark on it. If they cannot be with Terry as much as they would like, as least when they are with him they should let him know that they understand the problems he is having, and are proud of him as he makes some headway at solving them.

Mr. and Mrs. G. asked, however, how Terry can learn to correct his mistakes if they are not pointed out to him. In answer to this, the staff explained that all one learns when his mistakes are pointed out is that he has made mistakes; one learns to do something correctly only by being informed when his behavior is in the right direction.

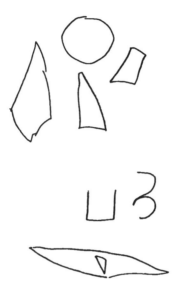

Figure 18. *Terry G.'s Bender Designs.*

Contrary to the common-sense adage, they were told, we learn only by "trial and success," not by "trial and error;" errors tell us only that we have done something wrong, not how to do it correctly; when we are told that what we have just done is a little better than average, we are at least able to repeat what we have just done, and if we keep repeating it, eventually we will do it even a little better, which again should be commented on.

Parents cannot help criticizing at times, they were told, and under the right circumstances criticisms may help; but a child can with certainty be set on the right course of action only when he is helped to recognize which among his many actions are the best ones to follow through on.

Mr. and Mrs. G. are well-educated and intelligent people, and seemed to quickly understand what the staff was trying to explain. They regretted, they said, that they had not realized these things sooner, and insisted that they were going to drastically alter their treatment of Terry.

The follow-up report of the public health nurse two years later is as follows:

> Terry repeated the first grade with a new first-grade teacher. This teacher took a special interest in Terry, and he did quite well.
>
> He did even better during the second grade, and is now going into the third grade. His mother says that he still sometimes rocks and hits his head, but he is gradually losing this habit. Actually the whole family is better; they have bought a camper and use it together quite frequently. Terry is no longer considered a discipline problem at school.

CHAPTER 10

Oppositionalism in Children with Learning Disabilities

As one becomes familiar with the kinds of behavioral effects parental pressure can produce in children, one learns to recognize many of the specific problems children have with learning in school as signs of oppositionalism. In their unconscious struggle to maintain their own individuality against parents who they feel would overwhelm them with their insatiable aspirations and anxieties, children acquire habits of doing just the opposite of what others attempt to get them to do. In school, therefore, they routinely have difficulties with the easiest of tasks, reverse concepts and procedures, cling to irrelevancies while ignoring essentials, and close their minds to simple and logical lines of reasoning.

There are, however, children with minimal brain dysfunction due to birth injury, convulsions in childhood associated with infectious disease and severe fever, or other specific mechanisms known to injure the developing brain, whose problems in learning may seem very similar to those manifested by oppositional children. Because of the similarity of their classroom failings, it is ordinarily quite difficult to distinguish learning-disabled children from those whose problems in learning are nothing more than aspects of their overall reactions to parental pressure.

Like the Oppositional Child, the learning-disabled child presents a paradoxical picture. Some learning tasks are quite easy for him, while other tasks, seemingly no more difficult, are nearly impossible. And not only are his capabilities drastically different from task to task, but his general level of ability seems to fluctuate drastically from one day to the next. And like oppositionalism, learning disabilities take many forms, with many different secondary emotional and intellectual reactions associated with them.

Many, if not most, children with learning disabilities experience difficulties in perceiving form and patterns. These disturbances in perception may be auditory, but are more commonly visual. The child may not immediately recognize a square as a square, especially if it is presented to him at a 45° angle, and as a result may not be able to draw it. He may confuse the figure in a drawing with the background, or he may not be able to grasp the sequence of letters or numbers in series.

It should not only be obvious that such perceptual difficulties seriously interfere with the ability to learn to read, write and do arithmetic, but it should be equally obvious that these kinds of difficulties in the learning-disabled look, at least superficially, very much like the kinds of difficulties oppositional children have.

The Oppositional Child, with his upside down or backward writing and drawings, his reversals of concepts and procedures, and his seemingly inexplicable difficulties with what should be simple tasks, may be misdiagnosed as learning-disabled. Or both the learning-disabled and the oppositional may be lumped together and labeled "dyslexic." And what is even more confusing is the fact that nearly all learning-disabled children are pressured by their parents, with the result that almost all learning-disabled children show not only difficulties in learning due to perceptual disturbances, but also difficulties in learning due to the oppositionalism they have developed as a defense against parental pressure.

Distinguishing Oppositionalism From Learning Disabilities

Disturbances in learning due to oppositionalism are more clearly evident the easier the task. The Oppositional Child, although unconscious of it, deliberately strives to defeat himself and to defeat those who are trying to teach him. This goal is easier to achieve the easier the task. The Oppositional Child, for example, is more likely to "misinterpret" directions (do the opposite of what he is told to do) when the directions are simple than when the directions are complex. The behavior of the learning-disabled child is entirely different; if the learning-disabled child can do the task at all, he will perform better the easier the task.

It is oppositional to do something exactly the wrong

way, but to do something exactly the wrong way is not always possible. One can do precisely the opposite of what one is supposed to do only when what one is supposed to do is obvious. Thus, on easy motor-perceptual tasks, for example, the Oppositional Child may produce beautiful figure-ground reversals, accurate upside-down or mirror drawing, perfect inversions of symbols and designs, and other effects precisely opposite of what is called for.

But on difficult motor-perceptual tasks, the Oppositional Child may be unable to maintain his oppositional set. He may "forget," and without realizing what he is doing, begin doing the difficult motor-perceptual tasks correctly. And when he cannot do the difficult motor-perceptual tasks correctly, his inability to maintain an oppositional set on the difficult tasks will result in his using more efficient techniques in attempting the difficult tasks than he uses in attempting the easy tasks.

Doing poorly on easy tasks while doing better on more difficult tasks is a peculiar paradox of oppositionalism. And although the effect learning disabilities have on behavior are often as paradoxical as those of oppositionalism, this particular paradox is *not* characteristic of learning disabilities.

It should be pointed out that showing marked disturbances on easy tasks, with improvement in performance as the tasks grow more difficult, is not only characteristic of the Oppositional Child on tests of motor-perceptive skills, but is also characteristic of him on other types of tests as well. On tests of information, immediate and delayed recall, arithmetic, social intelligence, and comprehension, the Oppositional Child typically misses the first few easy items while showing progressive improvement as the items become more difficult. Again this particular paradoxical pattern of performance, characteristic of oppositionalism, is not one ordinarily associated with learning disabilities.

The critical factor in the motor-perceptual disturbances of the learning-disabled which distinguishes them from those occurring in the oppositional is *confusion*. The learning-disabled child is *confused*; the Oppositional Child is not. The learning-disabled child confuses the top of the drawing with the bottom, the left side of the drawing with the right, and the sequence of letters or numbers in series. The learning-disabled child may draw the top of a figure correctly while reversing the bottom. He may draw both the right and the left half of a figure correctly, but put the left half of the drawing on the right and the right on the left. When he draws a figure backwards (a mirror drawing) he does not do so because he *sees* it backwards, nor, as the Oppositional Child, because he is compelled to draw it the opposite of how he sees it; the learning-disabled child draws a figure backwards because he has difficulty distinguishing backwards from forwards.

When the learning-disabled child draws a mirror-reversal, he does so by mistake; the Oppositional Child draws mirror-reversals by design. Relevant here is the fact that oppositional children can sometimes do better on a task when what is called for is a reversal. For example, oppositional children occasionally score higher on tests of immediate oral recall of numbers when they are instructed to repeat them in reverse (digits backward) than when instructed to recite them as given (digits forward).

Learning-disabled children, on the other hand, are just as confused, or even more so, when trying to recall numbers in a reverse order as when trying to recall them as given. In short, the learning-disabled child often feels defeated because he cannot tell when he has "things turned around," while the Oppositional Child often deliberately "turns things around" in order to defeat those who are trying to pressure him.

As was mentioned in Chapter 3, sometimes in setting out to draw a square or diamond, the Oppositional Child will, as he reaches a corner, impulsively move his pencil in exactly the wrong direction; in correcting the direction of these erroneous lines at each corner, he may produce projections which appear to be what psychologists call "ears."

The learning-disabled child sometimes also puts "ears" at he corners of the squares and diamonds he draws, but for entirely different reasons. The "ears" in the drawings of the learning-disabled child, unlike those in the drawings of the Oppositional Child, are signs of form-perception disturbance.

To a learning-disabled child, a square or diamond may not appear to be a square or diamond at all, but rather, because of his inability to perceive form, the square or diamond may be to him simply four straight lines connecting to four corners. The learning-disabled child then draws the figure as he sees it: he draws the four sides and then goes back and puts in the corners. It does not occur to the learning-disabled child that the two lines joined constitute a corner, and therefore he adds in a corner at each point where two lines meet; the additional corners he adds where two lines meet constitute his peculiar "ears."

With practice and instruction in copying designs and figures, the learning-disabled child can be led to realize that these "ears" are superfluous, and although only vaguely able to see this himself, can gradually learn to leave them out, at least on simple designs and figures. But on unfamiliar or complex designs and figures, the learning-disabled child's capacity to compensate for his faulty form perception frequently breaks down, and "ears," seemingly inexplicable to people without form-perception disturbances, appear in his drawings.

Just as the mirror reversals drawn by the learning-disabled are mistakes, the "ears" drawn by the oppositional are mistakes (conscientious oppositional children will erase them.) And just as the mirror reversals drawn by the oppositional are by design, the "ears" drawn by the learning-disabled are by design (learning-disabled children typically go back after the sides of the figure have been drawn and carefully add in the "ears").

The mistakes oppositional children make in their drawings are usually in some way or other reversals, but the child with learning disabilities makes other kinds of mistakes as well. For example, the learning-disabled child may draw a square as a four-pointed star, he may separate a single figure into two figures, or he may grotesquely bend a perfectly straight figure.

The explanation is that learning-disabled children are

unable to perceive form and patterns accurately, while
oppositional children perceive form and patterns accurately
but have acquired strong habits of doing exactly the
opposite of what is expected of them.

Pressuring the Learning-Disabled Child

Distinguishing between learning disabilities and
oppositionalism, although difficult, would be a great deal
easier were it not for the fact, as mentioned earlier, that
nearly all children with learning disabilities are relentlessly
pressured by their parents, with the effect that seldom does
one find a simple case of learning disability. In nearly all
cases of learning disability there is present a heavy overlay
of oppositionalism, developed by the learning-disabled child
as a defense against these parental pressures.

Pressuring a child with learning disabilities serves only
to magnify his difficulties and create self-defeating
oppositional reactions which further erode his capacity to
learn in school.

The pressured child with learning disabilities will regress
to lower and lower levels of achievement. He does not
know why he cannot learn as other children do, why
seemingly easy tasks often are for him so difficult, and why
what he is able to do one day becomes impossible the next.
Nor does he realize that his oppositional reactions to
parental pressure and criticism interfere with his capacity to
learn. But the more he feels pressured, the worse he does,

and the worse he does, the more hopeless he becomes. Parents of the learning-disabled child, on the other hand, *know* he could do better. They know this because on some tasks and on some days he does do better. They assume that when he does not do as well as they expect him to do, it is because he is not paying attention, or is lazy, and they see their job as one of having to keep after him. And thus the vicious cycle is set in motion: the more pressure the parents apply, the worse the child does; and the worse the child does, the more pressure the parents feel they must apply.

The point finally comes where the child's original learning disability is almost academic, so overriding have his difficulties due to oppositionalism become. Under such circumstances even the professional psychologist may find it puzzling as to whether or not, and to what extent, a learning disability is in fact present. And any learning disability present, as we have said, may be of little consequence in comparison to the severe emotional and learning problems brought on by oppositionalism.

In addition to specific motor-perceptual disturbances, most learning-disabled children, even when not pressured, manifest generally low tolerance for intense distracting stimuli. Not only are they unable to ignore such stimuli, but they are made increasingly nervous and tense when subjected to them for any lengthy period of time.

Forced to remain in a room for several hours with the static of a blaring radio, flickering fluorescent lights, or loudly argumentative people, learning-disabled children will often become either hyperactive, disoriented or simply exhausted. And this effect may last for the duration of the day and into the night, interfering with normal rest and sleep.

With their rest and sleep disturbed, these children awake the next morning sluggish and in a dazed condition, whereupon their parents must prod them repeatedly and speak loudly and harshly to them in order to get them off to school on time. Arriving at school following such circumstances, learning-disabled children are in no condition for effective learning, nor for recalling previously learned material and skills.

Again the similarity between learning disabilities and oppositionalism is striking. The sluggish, dazed behavior of the learning-disabled after a night of disturbed sleep may seem indistinguishable from the foot-dragging delaying tactics of the oppositional. And the fact that learning-disabled children, like other children, acquire oppositional traits as a result of the persistent harassment by their parents makes their behavior and that of children whose only problem is oppositionalism even more similar.

With oppositional traits such as hostility, depression, alienation, feelings of inferiority, and affectional anxiety present, it may be difficult to discern that underneath these traits is a learning disability. Even serious motor-perceptual disturbances due to minimal brain dysfunction can be dwarfed by pervasive habit disturbances associated with oppositionalism.

Minor learning disabilities, on the other hand, may appear extremely severe when accompanied by well-established and long-standing habits of oppositionalism. In any case, whenever learning disabilities are accompanied by heavy overlays of oppositionalism, reducing parental pressures is always a necessary first step in assessing the severity and extent of the learning disabilities.

Removing the Pressures

Although it may be difficult to distinguish learning-disabled children with oppositional traits from oppositional children without learning disabilities, the action needed on the part of the parents under both circumstances is not difficult. Whenever oppositionalism is present, whether there are learning disabilities present or not, the action needed is that rather than criticizing and pressuring their children, parents should begin supporting their children by noticing and commenting on their best efforts and their small daily achievements.

With the removal of pressure, and with the introduction of support, both the learning-disabled and the children without learning disabilities no longer need to waste their intellect and mental energies in pointless struggles to salvage their egos from overzealous parents. They are therefore freed to use their abilities to the maximum in tackling the problems of learning.

The problem of the learning-disabled child with oppositional traits is no different from that of other oppositional children. Before he can discover and use to the fullest his abilities to learn, he must rid himself of self-defeating oppositionalism. The more severe his learning disabilities, the more crucial it is that he use what abilities he has to the maximum. In order for him to use his abilities to the maximum, it is necessary that his parents give him the support and encouragement he needs.

When the learning-disabled child has bad days, his parents should commiserate. *"You had a bad day, eh? I know how that can be;"* or *"I'm so sorry it went bad for you today, maybe tomorrow will be better."* When he has good days, they should share with him the jobs of small achievements. *"Say, that's one of the best arithmetic papers you've had! Congratulations,"* or *"Look at all those words you spelled correct! You're getting to be a better speller all the time."* And at no time should the parents fuss at him or nag him about the fact he should be doing better.

If parents can give encouragement, they will be surprised at the abilities even the severely learning-disabled child can demonstrate. If they cannot give encouragement, but can only criticize and pressure their child, then it will not matter what abilities their child may possess, for he will never be able to demonstrate them. At least he will never demonstrate them at a time or place where his parents can see them.

Illustrative Case
Allen H.

Allen is nine years old and is in the third grade. He was referred by his teacher because he is doing poorly in school and is a discipline problem. He is the oldest of three children. Mr. and Mrs. H. are both high school graduates, and both are employed.

The report from his teacher states that Allen seems capable of doing better work in school than he actually does, and when on rare occasions he applies himself, he is very proud of his achievement. Most of the time he is inattentive, *"Just stares into space"*, is often confused, and often misbehaves. *"He never looks at you when you speak to him,"* the report states, *"And he seems very disturbed at times."* The report goes on to say that he rebels and sulks when corrected, does not bring in his assignments, and is very reluctant to take home papers and report cards with low grades on them.

The psychologist's report is as follows:

> On the Wechsler Intelligence Scale for children, Allen demonstrated a verbal IQ of 101, a Performance IQ of 83, and a Full Scale IQ of 92. His fund of information, judgment, immediate recall, critical accuracy at routine paper-and-pencil tasks are all average. His ability to plan ahead is poor, and his form perception is extremely disturbed.
>
> On the Wechsler, he had difficulty with directions, due to rigidity, involuntary negativism, and impulsiveness. Although many of his answers were disorganized, idiosyncratic, and difficult to score, there is ample evidence of normal intelligence. But there seem to be mild brain damage and severe emotional problems present.
>
> His drawings reveal frustration, hostility and the feeling that pressures are being placed on him greater than he can handle. His drawings indicate severe

emotional problems, the separations and loss of form indicating brain damage.

He presents a rich, volatile, disorganized Rorschach indicating uncontrolled impulsivity and intense stress. There is a paranoid flavor to his adjustment and he feels that others are against him, but despite the vigorous impulsivity and bizarre ideation, ties to reality seem to be sound at the present time. But he is confused and frightened by reality and by his internal impulses, and he escapes into illogical fantasy. It disrupts his thought processes and his self-control. As he is going now it is difficult to see how he can avoid eventually developing at least a marginal schizophrenia.

On the Wide Range Achievement Test, he demonstrated sight-reading at the 2.8 grade level and arithmetic at the 3.1 grade level.

Conclusion: A severely emotionally disturbed boy with normal intelligence whose thought processes and self-control are disturbed due, in part, to mild brain damage. This boy needs therapy and special tutoring, and his parents need help in working through the problems. Unless effort is made to alter the direction of his present maladjustive tendencies, he most certainly is headed toward even more severe maladjustment.

The results of the psychological tests were discussed with Mr. and Mrs. H. They seemed interested in all that was said, and appeared anxious to do what is best for their child. The fact that Allen has specific learning disabilities due to some sort of minimal brain dysfunction was discussed with them. The particular sort of difficulties Allen has in learning, and how his difficulties have been made much worse by the pressures he feels he is under, were explained to them.

Support was given to the parents for the many positive factors in their family situation, but they were told that Allen needs more encouragement for what he tries to do, and less criticism. Mr. H., who works hard and sets high standards for himself, could not at first see how letting up on Allen would be good for him, but gradually he began to understand Allen's problems from the child's point of view, and helped his wife understand.

It was emphasized to them that they were not to fuss at Allen when he had bad days, and to be sure to notice and to comment when he does anything a little better than he ordinarily does. Mrs. H., who is inclined to do too many things for Allen and tends to reinforce immature behavior in him, was advised to let Allen do more things on his own.

The idea of concentrating on Allen's good behavior and ignoring as much as possible his bad behavior seemed to be quite novel to Mr. and Mrs. H., and it took quite a lengthy discussion in order for them to accept the idea.

At the session's end, the parents seemed to understand the kinds of things they needed to do, and agreed to return for further discussions as the need arose.

Two months later, Mrs. H. returned for a follow-up interview. She brought three of Allen's spelling papers on which he had made two C's and a B+ and showed them with great pride. She said that Allen's grades have been much better, and that they have been pinning his best school papers up in the living room.

She said that she and Mr. H. had discussed their

Figure 19. *Allen H.'s Draw-A-Person (at age 9).*

interview after they got home from the clinic, and had discussed it with Allen. Since then everyone had made a real effort. She said that she realized that the attitudes of all three of them, and the other children, have an interlocking effect. She had managed to let Allen do more things for himself, and her husband had relaxed his strict standards. Both she and her husband, she said, began noticing and remarking when Allen behaved well, and Allen's behavior had improved overall, not only in school.

   "We are all so much more relaxed with each other," she said, *"I can hardly believe it is the same family."*

   Two years later Allen was referred again to the clinic by

the school for possible Special Class placement. The principal of the school in requesting a psychological re-evaluation stated that Allen seemed no longer to be emotionally disturbed, nor was he a behavior problem, and he now seemed to get along well with other children. Allen was not, however, progressing satisfactorily in school. His teacher felt that Allen needed special help in learning.

Mrs. H. was seen before this re-evaluation. She stated that all was still well at home. Mrs. H. was still tactful and patient with Allen, she was still allowing him more freedom, and Allen, in turn, was becoming increasingly responsible. She was still enthusiastic about the change that had taken place in their lives since the first interview.

Figure 20. *Allen H.'s Bender Drawings (at age 9).*

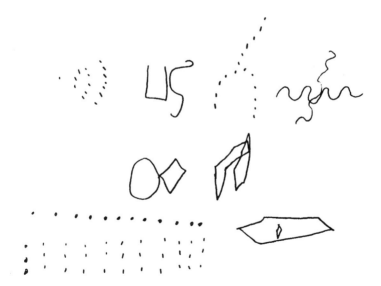

The psychological re-evaluation report which follows reveals that although there is generally marked improvement in Allen's emotional adjustment, his IQ scores have dropped approximately 10 points. The seriousness of Allen's learning disability is clearly evident now that his emotional problems have been largely alleviated. It is hoped that with his new-found self confidence and with special instruction he may achieve the maximum of which he is capable.

At the present time Allen is in the 5th grade. On the Wechsler Intelligence Scale for Children, he now demonstrates a Verbal IQ of 89, a Performance IQ of 76, and a Full Scale IQ of 81. His raw scores on the subtests were in general only a little improved over the previous testing, and the failure to increase these subtest scores at the expected rate causes his IQ scores to be lower.

His raw score on the Similarities subtest is actually lower than before, but this seems primarily due to greater self-control and less random guessing. His raw score on the Mazes is also a little lower, and this seems due to his now much greater attempts to control impulsivity; his inability to successfully control impulsivity slows his responses and causes him to finally give up. Previously he showed no such concern about his impulsivity.

At the present testing, Allen behaved in a mature manner, understood directions easily, not talking to himself as he did before, and showing none of the rigidity and negativism that he showed previously. There is, however, no change in the kinds of problems he has in perceiving form. In fact, his more mature test-taking behavior makes it easier to observe the difficulties he has in controlling impulsivity and in perceiving form.

On the Wide Range Achievement Test, he demonstrated reading at the 3.4 grade level and arithmetic at the 3.9 grade level. His academic achievement, like his intelligence, has not improved at the rate one might have expected in terms of his previous evaluation.

His Draw-A-Person and Bender drawings, while still revealing significant form-perception disturbances, are generally improved. He still shows signs that he feels pressured to achieve more academically and socially than he comfortably can, but he shows greater control of impulsivity, more maturity, better emotional balance, less hostility, and less depression.

The Rorschach reveals good reality ties and fairly sound ego-strengths and inner emotional resources. If under too much stress or frustration, his ability to cope will still collapse, but he is markedly better able now to absorb stress and frustration.

Although still somewhat aggressively competitive with others, he is now able to form both casual and deeply empathic friendships with his peers. He now shows no signs of paranoid feelings.

He is still cautious toward his father, but deep affection for his father is evident. He now shows a good capacity to relate empathically toward his mother. He is still having difficulty in making a masculine identification, still had difficulty in controlling aggressive tendencies, and is still generally unable to understand himself or the world around him. He has not as yet developed full personal ambition, but he feels he is making progress.

Conclusion: This re-evaluation reveals that Allen's general emotional adjustment has markedly improved. He is now exerting strong and mature efforts to control his impulsivity and aggressiveness. Depression is no

Figure 21. *Allen H.'s Draw-A-Person (at age 11).*

longer present, and he now shows good capacity for
empathy and affection, and reasonably sound ego-
strengths. Too much stress and frustration still
overwhelms him, but his tolerance level has markedly
increased.

The basic cause of his difficulties with impulsivity
is clearly minimal brain dysfunction, and faulty form-
perception results from this cause also. He is having
to use a significant amount of his mental energies in
controlling impulsivity, and the caution involved lowers
his usable intelligence. It is very likely that his
intellectual abilities will improve to the low normal
level as his new-found emotional adjustments become
habitual. But he will probably always have to be

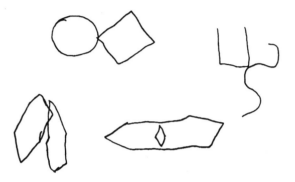

Figure 22. *Allen H.'s Bender Drawings (at age 11).*

intellectually cautious and slow in order to maintain a reliable level of achievement, and thus his scores on intelligence, abilities, and achievement tests will always be below average.

It may be that due to the minimal brain dysfunction specific areas of his mental development may be impaired, but at present only his form-perception seems impaired. This impairment will undoubtedly cause him to have difficulties in reading, spelling, and writing, but compensatory habits of special effort and caution, as he now manifests, can at least partially overcome the handicaps created by his form-perception impairment. In such a case, progress in school may be slow, but the fundamental academic skills can be mastered. It seems his parents and teachers have done an excellent job of improving their treatment of Allen. He clearly needs and could profit from special education services.

CHAPTER 11

High School and College Dropouts

In recent years there has been a progressive increase in the number of bright students who for non-economic and non-health reasons abandon their education before reaching the goals set for themselves. It seems sometimes that *only* the bright students are dropping out, while the mediocre are plodding on to completion. If oppositionalism is serving as a main contributor to this situation, then we should expect that many dropouts will return to complete their educations later, after having successfully escaped from parental pressures. And this is exactly what is happening; adults are returning to college in larger numbers now than ever before.

The fact that these older returnees often are better students than their younger classmates, having greater seriousness of purpose and bringing to their studies greater maturity and experience, makes this state of affairs not at all calamitous. But what is near calamitous is the anxiety of many of these older students.

Bright adults who did not finish high school may take the General Educational Development Test, a test of high school equivalency, and if they pass, are allowed to go directly to college. Those who were formerly in college but dropped out may, of course, return to college whenever they desire to and are financially able.

Most of these former high school and college dropouts take up their studies anew with extreme trepidation, and for many of them their concern is not that they may not do well, but that they may not excel. As one professor put it, *"These adult students, more often than not, kill flies with sledge hammers!"* Older students typically undertake their first introductory or survey courses in college as if the task set for them were to master an entire field in one semester, or as if their entire career rested on one test (or even one question of one test).

Under such self-imposed pressures, their professors must take time to help alleviate some of their onerous anxieties and reassure them that perfection is not expected of them. On test days many of these older students come to class exhausted and trembling to agonize over the test questions. They are angered or humiliated if, when their papers are returned graded a few days later, any of their answers have been marked wrong. And, paradoxically, if all their answers are marked correct and their papers given top grades, they not infrequently make disparaging comments among themselves about the low standards of the course and its lack of challenge. In the light of how anxiously perfectionistic many of these older students are when resuming their education, one can imagine how even more anxious they must have been when they dropped out.

Of course, most of these older, returning students would probably claim that when they were young they were not nearly so anxious as now, that their fear now is that during the ensuing years since they were in school they have "forgotten" how to study.

But it is more likely that if they were less anxious when young than now, it is only because as teenagers and young adults they were never really applying themselves. Had they done so, had they applied themselves then as they are doing now, without their present maturity and experience to temper their outlook, they undoubtedly would have been a great deal more anxious than now. And considering the degree of stress they appear to be under now, it is reasonable to assume that they did not apply themselves then because it would have been far too stressful to do so. Thus it was under the threat of an even greater stress than they are experiencing now that they had dropped out of school.

Thus in the emotional reactions of these anxiously perfectionistic older students one sees something of what many of today's young high school and college students are threatened with. Conditioned to believe that whatever they may achieve will never equal the lofty aspirations their parents have for them, that whatever they do will only reveal how much more they should do, these pressured young people may avoid trying altogether.

Constantly told that they could always do better, their ultimate goals in life seem vague and amorphous. Feeling that only great and glorious accomplishments would be worthy of them, they spurn the mundane tasks which their education demands, with no idea what the first steps toward these great accomplishments should be. They feel blocked and uncertain, frustrated, anxious, and depressed.

On many occasions, particularly after stimulating late-night discussions with friends, they go to bed resolving to undertake worthwhile projects tomorrow; but in the morning for some reason the incentive is gone, and they usually cannot even recall precisely what it was that they were going to do. As a result they drag themselves out of bed only to begin another day of procrastination.

"I've been a loser all my life," is a remark one hears from healthy, robust, attractive, and intelligent young people, and one cannot but be astounded at this incredible self-deception, this blatant distortion of the facts.

If anything, these fortunate young people are winners; but winners, strangely enough, who cannot exploit their advantages. The opportunities afforded them are to them terrifying. What if they tried, what if they *really* tried, and fell short? What would people think of them? And worst yet, what if they really tried and did not excel, what would they think of themselves?

The typical high school and college dropout begins dropping out long before he actually quits attending class altogether. Because he gains so little satisfaction from his educational activities, the most minimal effort at class attendance or study becomes extremely taxing for him. He feels listless and bored.

He wants to excel in his studies and seek the plaudits he has come to believe he has the right to seek, but he is afraid to try. He does not know why he is afraid to try; or rather he knows in part why; he knows secretly, but dares not admit it, that he fears he may not actually have the ability his parents have led him to believe he has.

His parents have told him repeatedly, since he was a small child, that if he just applied himself he could do wonders. He may have applied himself in the primary grades, but as he progressed in school excelling became more and more difficult.

The further along in school he gets before he begins to doubt his abilities, the more disruptive these doubts are. If he made excellent grades in elementary school, it is disgraceful to be able to make only B's in junior high and high school; and if he made straight A's in high school, he should expect to do the same in college. As he begins to fear that he cannot with certainty come up to his own and his parents expectations, he avoids applying himself to the maximum.

By not applying himself, he has a ready-made, ego-salvaging explanation for why he does not excel. But the less he applies himself, the lower his grades become and the less gratifying is his school work. And the less pleasurable gratification he gains from his school work, the more difficult it is to apply himself. Perhaps a formerly excellent student, but now headed downhill academically unless something drastic redirects the course of events, he will soon be working far below his capacity, and will very likely leave school long before reaching his academic objectives.

Of course, he may have never applied himself, not even in elementary school. He may have learned from the first never to risk possible failure. In such a case, his supposedly superior academic ability has always been something of a family myth with perhaps little that is factual to support it.

But whether there is or is not some factual basis for

believing that he is academically brilliant, the long awaited moment when he must finally prove himself lies before him as some sort of dreaded and bitter end. He cannot possibly win at such a moment, for he knows that no matter what he might achieve he could never realize his parents' and his own naively unrealistic expectations.

But he could lose, he could easily fall shockingly short. Facing such a certain and disastrous fate, finding ego-saving reasons for dropping out of school before this fate overtakes him, becomes for him the only alternative.

"It's so boring in school," he says. *"My classes don't challenge me. I can find nothing that interests me. It's all memorization, with no opportunity to be creative."* And more of the same.

What produces these unreasonably high self-expectations? And why are the students who harbor them so often ill-prepared for pursuing reasonable academic objectives? Why does the situation become exactly the opposite of what the parents are striving to attain, and the exact opposite of what the young people themselves want? Why do so many capable, ambitious students, with every desire to do well in college, find themselves moving away from their most cherished dreams and away from their most strongly held life goals?

It is oppositional to drop out of school when one's chief goals in life require education. And the causes of oppositionalism are always the same, namely, pressure and criticism.

Everyone, whether it be a child in elementary school or a student in high school or college, wants to be noticed, admired, and loved. And any behavior which gets these rewards will be repeated. If his daily efforts at reading, writing, and arithmetic gain the child in elementary school parental support and praise, he will continue to apply himself.

But if his daily efforts go unnoticed and his best efforts are disparaged, he will find it more and more difficult to make these efforts. This does not mean that he has lost the desire to be someone special in his parents' eyes. On the contrary, the desire may be greater than ever. But when he finds it harder to apply his best efforts to his school work, it means that he has lost hope of attaining a special place in the eyes of his parents by conscientiously applying himself to such things as daily lessons in reading, writing, and arithmetic.

"How can he learn," asks the concerned father or mother, *"if we don't point out his mistakes?"* But all a child learns when his mistakes are pointed out to him is that he made mistakes, and is therefore undeserving of recognition for his efforts. What he needs is for his correct responses to be pointed out to him. He needs help in identifying when he has done something better than he usually does so that he can know to do more of that.

"But he will be satisfied to do poor or mediocre work," his parents argue, *"if we praise what he has done without showing him that he could do it better."* But the child knows the task could be done better, and if he is given recognition for what he has done, he will do it better. From his small successes will come bigger successes, but if he is always told that his first efforts are unsatisfactory, he has nothing on which to

build later successes.

Many parents withhold recognition from a child's initially small achievements by conveying to him that anything he does should be done in a superior manner. *"If it's worth doing at all, it's worth doing right,"* they say, implying that it is all right for other children to have mistakes in their work, but not he. In a sense they are telling their child that it is better to neglect his studies or to do failing work than to be mediocre.

Yet whenever any of us undertakes a new field or level of work we are very likely to do it at first only passably. And all of us hit plateaus where no matter how hard we try we cannot seem to improve.

The child who is led to believe that his effort should always and immediately produce superior results is misadvised and ill-prepared to tackle really challenging educational tasks. And the more convinced he is of this erroneous assumption, the more educational tasks he has to avoid in order to maintain a belief in his superiority.

To produce an eventual school dropout, the process is simple: first and foremost convince the child early in life that he is intellectually superior; and second, let him know that whatever he does is never really worthy of him. Such a combination makes certain that he can seldom really enjoy any academic achievement, and the person who seldom enjoys his achievements will sooner or later stop achieving.

Do this to a child and you can be reasonably sure that although his greatest desire in the world is to excel academically and thus justify his parents' faith in him, he will abandon his studies long before this goal is reached.

What's Wrong With C's?

When a son or daughter goes to college, and sometimes even to high school, the parents may feel threatened by the fact that much of what their child is learning is beyond or outside of the parents' own experience. Because of their poor or limited education the parents may feel uncertain concerning his or her progress, and feel too unsure of themselves to attempt to recognize their child's achievements.

But many a father and mother of poor or limited education have been powerful reinforcers of their children's efforts in college. Suppose, for example, a student whose parents have only a limited education comes home discouraged from college with only C's for his first semester's work. If the parents wish to encourage him they can point out that there is nothing wrong with C's, that gaining C's means that he has passed his first semester and that he can, if he continues to do as well, eventually graduate.

"You're the first person in this family to go to college," they might say, *"and your parents have not been able to provide you with very much in the way of educational background. . .but you made it through the first semester, and without making a single unsatisfactory grade!"*

The student who gets this kind of encouragement may be hesitant to accept it, but he will return to college with renewed confidence and hope, knowing that his parents support him and are proud of him. And the chances are he will make some B's the next semester. But if his parents, because of their lack of education, feel that they cannot praise his achievement then he is left alone with his discouragement, taking it back to college with him where it can only harm his chances of doing well the next semester.

When the parents themselves have been to college and know something of the frustrations and disappointments their child may face, they should be able to be more specific in the kinds of encouragements they give. And no matter how successful the parents may have been in college, they can always recall difficulties which they had, and there is no better time than when their child is discouraged to share these recollections with him.

The student who is led to believe that he has succeeded in courses only when he makes A's in them is less likely to find rewards in high school or college than one who considers C's to some extent successes. Of course, no one is as happy with C's as he is with A's, but to consider C's as failures is terribly self-defeating.

It should be obvious that the student with C's who, because of this, considers himself a failure in high school or college, is more likely to drop out than the student who considers C's as successes. Furthermore, the student with C's who can think of these grades as indicating some degree of success will probably increase his grades, for success has a way of breeding success.

If despite encouragements a student should feel, however, that he wants to drop out of high school or college, he should not be pressured or bribed to stay in. The alternatives should be discussed with him, and the consequences of his actions objectively considered. But the decision should be his to make. Parents should discipline themselves to realize this, and to remember that the student who leaves school because at the time he finds it too unrewarding or stressful, will very likely resume his studies later.

There is certainly nothing to be gained from continuing when one is getting very little out of it. Under such circumstances, it makes more sense to drop out and return at a time when one is better able to cope with the stresses involved and is better able to discover the rewards to be gained.

Illustrative Case
Roger L.

Mr. and Mrs. L. sought the advice of a psychiatrist because Roger is not progressing satisfactorily in school. Roger dropped out of high school while in the 10th grade, and stayed out for nearly a year. During the time he was out of school he worked at many odd jobs, each of them only briefly.

He has returned to high school now, but is doing near-failing work. He made excellent grades in elementary school, but his grades began to go down in junior high school. Roger is eighteen years of age, and is an only child. His parents are both college graduates with good records in college, and his father is an outstanding member of his profession. The psychiatrist referred Roger to a psychologist for evaluation of his intelligence and personality, and the psychological report is as follows:

> On the Wechsler Adult Intelligence Scale, Roger demonstrated a Verbal IQ of 121, a Performance IQ of 123 and a Full Scale IQ of 123. These scores indicate "superior" intelligence.
>
> The personality material suggests a basically well-adjusted individual with a high degree of perfectionism and strong fears of failure. The perfectionism causes him to be very critical of his own achievements and to expect more of himself than he can possibly accomplish. The fear of failure produces anxiety and depression whenever he starts a new and difficult undertaking, for he has learned that he may not come up to his own expectations. The anxiety and depression lower his efficiency and cause his achievement to be below his true ability. This produces even more depression and anxiety, and he feels he is a disappointment not only to himself but to his parents as well.
>
> Depression and anxiety slow down his intellectual speed and interfere with concentration. This cycle is, of course, difficult to break, but must be broken soon if he is going to achieve in his present high school work.
>
> It appears that he has the basic ego strengths for overcoming this problem with time, but he needs to be making progress now. He does not allow himself to find rationalizations or excuses for his lack of self-confidence, and although this basic honesty is difficult to bear, it is the main reason one can be certain that he will eventually work through this problem.
>
> It appears that Roger is a product of perfectionistic parents. The father probably sets high standards for the boy, and the mother while overprotecting him also

expects much of him. He is overwhelmed by his parents, cannot come up to the standards they set for him, and feels constantly threatened by their achievements.

Emotionally he is in an impossible situation. He cannot win; he can only lose. Under the circumstances, the fact that he is depressed and anxious is not only normal but healthy.

Four years later, the psychologist received a letter from Roger giving a brief history of himself since he had last seen the psychologist and asking him, if he would, to please write a letter of recommendation for him to the admissions director of an exclusive private university.

Roger stated that he had graduated from high school, *"just barely,"* he said, and had enlisted in the Army where he had qualified for officers training, eventually becoming a First Lieutenant in the Infantry. He was now out of the Army and wished to resume his studies, and he hoped that his high school grades would not keep him out of this private university.

The psychologist wrote the letter requested, briefly describing Roger's level of intelligence and previous emotional problems concerning school, and urged the admissions director to give Roger a chance despite his poor showing in high school.

The psychologist heard no more from Roger until, five years later, he met him by chance at a meeting of public school personnel. Roger informed him at that time that he had not been admitted to the private college, but had attended a state university graduating in Education with certificates to teach English and Social Studies.

He was now teaching in a high school. He preferred, he said, teaching English, but due to the shortage of positions, he was teaching Social Studies. He was going to night school and summer school working toward his Master's degree. He was married now, he said, and his wife was also a teacher. They had no children.

The last question the psychologist asked him was, *"And how are your grades?"* Roger smiled. *"I make mostly A's,"* he said.

CHAPTER 12

Unmaking Oppositionalism

Oppositionalism is terribly wasteful and totally unnecessary. It is easy to avoid making a child oppositional, but if we have not avoided doing so, there is still no reason why we cannot undo the harm we have done by changing the way we treat the child.

To prevent or remove oppositionalism in a child, the parent need not alter his complete personality nor try to be a different person. All that he needs to do is relax the pressure he is imposing on the child, and from time to time, comment favorably on something the child has done which is a little better than he usually does.

The parent need not even stop criticizing. If he must criticize, the only thing he need remember is not to mix criticisms with favorable comments, for to do so nullifies the positive effects of the favorable comments. He can, however, mix favorable comments with his criticism if he wishes, for to do so often makes the criticism more acceptable.

Although criticisms are less harsh when preceded or followed by favorable comments, they nevertheless remain criticisms. And criticisms, no matter how well-intentioned nor how mild, do not help a child find pleasure in what he is doing. Criticisms may for the moment cause a child to improve his school work and behavior, but he is doing so only to avoid further criticisms, and if he improved only to avoid criticisms, the foundation for later oppositionalism has been laid.

A child, if he is not to become oppositional, must once in a while hear favorable comments completely devoid of any criticisms.

And the child of even the most obstinate, impatient, selfish, and thoughtless parent can be free of oppositionalism if the parent, at least some of the time, gives free and unadulterated credit when credit is due.

But if a parent feels that he must wait until his child has achieved some preconceived level of excellence before he will comment favorably, if he holds back praise for fear the child will be content with second-rate performance, if he feels that any recognition he gives must, for the child's own good, always be tempered with critical observations on how the child could improve, then he will see oppositionalism grow steadily in his child though the parent could be otherwise a paragon of virtue.

The earlier the parent attempts to overcome oppositionalism in his child, the better. It is always easier to prevent oppositionalism than to get rid of it after it has become an established pattern. But it is never too late to be effective, if the parent sincerely desires to be. Even teenagers, who are notoriously prone to remain oppositional long after there is any need to be, will eventually abandon their oppositionalism if their parents do not lose heart and, despite the teenager's seeming imperviousness, persist in recognizing good actions and behaviors while refraining from the use of pressure.

Rewarding Best Responses

There are few things a child can do perfectly the first time he attempts them, but he needs encouragement at the first more than any other stage of learning. Psychologists recommend at the outset of learning the method of *successive approximation* or *shaping* in which the ultimate goal of learning is not sought at the first, but rather the child is praised for the closest approximations he can make to the ultimate goal, regardless of how far short of the ultimate goal his best responses fall.

In the first grade, Junior always brought his papers home for his parents to see. His father, in looking over these papers, made a practice of noting what Junior had done well. The father tended to ignore any poor work or mistakes, and when Junior called his attention to his failings he would say, *"Yes, but look what a fine job you did here,"* pointing out something Junior had done especially well. Junior enjoyed school, enjoyed showing his school papers to his parents, and in general showed steady improvement throughout the year.

As an example of the effect that his father's treatment had on Junior, on one occasion when his father was looking over Junior's papers he noticed a sample of his son's penmanship which was for him exceptionally good. Junior's penmanship up to then had not been particularly noteworthy, but this particular sample of writing was very good. *"Did you write this?"* his father asked. When his son said he did, the father said, *"This is excellent! I didn't know you could write so well!"*

The father handed the paper to his wife who was equally impressed. Junior, proud of being the cause of such comments, moved to his mother's side so that he could look over her shoulder as she examined his writing. *"That is very good,"* she said. *"Every letter is nicely formed."*

Junior's penmanship improved throughout the first grade. Occasionally his parents would remark on this fact, and by the end of the year he was receiving "outstanding" on his report card for penmanship. Junior is now in high school and his penmanship is still exceptionally good.

Using the method of successive approximation is obviously necessary for the first grader in his initial attempts at reading, writing, and arithmetic, but it is also necessary later in school whenever a child's achievement has fallen behind that of his classmates. Encouraging a child to overcome his learning deficiencies begins by recognizing his best responses, no matter how poor they may appear in comparison to those of his classmates.

Tim, who had never made very good grades in school, was now in the fifth grade and was failing spelling. His father, who had always believed in the traditional methods of pointing out mistakes and drilling, decided to change his tactics.

One day when Tim brought home one of his spelling papers with an F on it, his father looked at the paper and commented on the words Tim had spelled correctly.

"I've always had trouble with spelling myself," he confessed, *"but you have some words spelled correctly here that I am not sure I always spell correctly."* And the father proceeded to read aloud all the words which Tim had spelled correctly.

"That's really not bad," he said, *"but I guess your teacher wants you to do better. Let's keep our fingers crossed, and hope you can do better."*

Each time Tim brought home F papers in spelling, his father commiserated with him and commented only on the words Tim had spelled correctly, and finally the day came when Tim brought home a spelling paper with a D on it.

"Hey!" his father exclaimed, upon seeing the paper, *"You've broken the jinx! You made a D! Now that's something we ought to celebrate. Go get your mother and your little brother, and tell them we're going to the drive-in for hamburgers and milk shakes because you raised your grade in spelling."*

Although Tim still brought home F's in spelling, most of his papers were now D's. And then one day, he happily greeted his father with a C spelling paper, and again the family celebrated with hamburgers and milk shakes at the drive-in.

When Tim finally brought home a B spelling paper, and later an A paper, there were even bigger celebrations, and, of course, Tim passed spelling, having no more difficulties with this subject throughout his years in school. And his father, in the meantime, became an ardent believer in the effectiveness of rewarding best responses.

The method of successive approximation is as effective in eliminating bad habits as it is in the acquisition of good ones. In the following example, fingernail biting, a form of oppositional behavior usually extremely difficult to get rid of, was effectively overcome by rewarding best responses.

Carol, who was in the fifth grade, came to her parents' bedroom one afternoon and, seeing her mother alone, announced with chagrin, *"Mom, I've been biting my fingernails lately, and I can't seem to stop myself from doing it."*

Carol reached her hands out showing her mother bitten nails. Her mother looked them over carefully, and said, *"You haven't bitten them all. The nails on the little fingers of each hand are not bitten, and these next to them are only bitten a little."*

Saying this, the mother took Carol over to her dressing table and got out her fingernail file and polish. *"Let's see if we can shape these nails that haven't been bitten,"* she said, *"and make them pretty."* She worked awhile on Carol's nails, filing them and then polishing them. *"The nails of your little fingers look very nice now. There's not much we can do with the rest, but at least we can make these look pretty."*

The next day Carol's mother purchased a fingernail kit for Carol, and in the weeks that followed, she and Carol did their fingernails together. Carol did not immediately stop biting her nails, but with only a few disappointing setbacks, she gradually bit her nails less and less. By the middle of the next school year Carol was no longer biting her nails at all, and had beautifully cared-for nails. No one ever told Carol to stop biting her nails; no one lectured her, no one threatened her, and no one became upset about the fact that she bit her nails. Carol is now in college, and still has beautifully cared-for nails.

Letting Oppositional Behavior Exhaust Itself

Though it is never too late for the parent to alter his relationship with his child, the older the child is the more limited are the parent's resources for effecting change, and the slower can changes be brought about. When oppositional conflicts between parent and child are of long duration and are well-established, frequently the only alternative is to let the child's oppositionalism run its course. Psychologists call this approach the exhaustion method. If this method is used, the parent must refrain from any criticism and abstain from using pressure, and while commenting on whatever the child does that he can approve of, patiently wait for the child to abandon his self-defeating behavior.

As he waits for his child's oppositionalism to exhaust itself, the parent should examine his own behavior, to be sure that he is not inadvertently reinforcing the child's oppositionalism. For example, the parent should not let himself become enraged by his son or daughter's oppositional behavior, for causing a parent to become emotionally upset is often gratifying to the Oppositional Child: to counteract his tendency to become upset, the parent should sincerely try to see the good that is being achieved by his son's or daughter's behavior, and not view it as more harmful than it actually is. And the parent should quietly remove financial support for a teenager or young adult who has dropped out of school when he is perfectly capable of supporting himself.

The most difficult task the parent has, if he has pressured and criticized his child for many years, is overcoming his own long-established habits. The biggest obstacle the parent must overcome in attempting to rid a teenager or young adult of oppositionalism is not the child's behavior, but his own. The parent must recognize that the problem behavior that first needs changing is his own, that he must change how he treats the child if there is ever to be a change in the child's behavior. But this task is not quite as formidable as it might appear, for the parent need not achieve perfection in order for the child to change. All that is needed in order for the child to change is for the parent to want to change; when the child is finally convinced that the parent is trying to change and is no longer dedicated to pressuring him, when he sees that his parent is not trying to place blame on him but is sincerely looking for the good in him, he usually gives up his oppositionalism.

> Calvin was a straight-A student when he dropped out of his sophomore year in college to join a commune. His father was a successful businessman who had always driven himself and his son to achieve to the maximum, but after a long, soul-searching talk with a psychologist about his son, the father decided that it would be unwise to try to force his son to come back to college.
>
> For a while the father did nothing. After about four months, he wrote to his son asking if he could come for a visit to the commune. In his letter the father assured his son that he had no intention of trying to persuade him to come back to college, and in his answer the son agreed, though somewhat reluctantly, to his father's visit. The father took a week off from work, and

arrived at the commune dressed appropriately in outdoor clothes.

The father spent nearly the entire week at the commune. During his stay he made no statements disparaging or ridiculing his son or the members of the commune or what they were attempting to do, nor did he offer any suggestions or advice. Rather, he watched and listened, and whenever anything seemed to be done well or seemed to be particularly worthwhile he mentioned the fact. While there the father did not participate in any activity which would have been contrary to his own moral values or would have been inappropriate for his age and position with them, but he did not criticize what they did.

At first the young people in the commune, including his son, were apprehensive in his presence, but gradually they relaxed. The father found that there were many things he liked about their life. For example, he particularly liked their homemade bread, and the young woman who baked it seemed pleased. By the time the father was to leave he was truly enjoying himself. He and his son had talked more together than they had ever done before. Although there had been some awkward moments, and some of the members of the commune had persisted throughout his visit in remaining aloof, he had formed friendships.

As he was getting into his car to leave, the young woman who regularly did the baking gave him a package with three loaves of her bread in it, and several members of the commune expressed regret that he had to leave so soon and asked him to come for another visit.

At home he wrote to his son often asking specific questions about things that were happening at the commune. His son answered with long, informative letters to which were usually added postscripts by others in the commune. The father felt closer to his son now than he had ever felt when he was at home. A year later the son gave up the commune life, returned to college and finished his studies in good order, going into a business career very similar to that of his father. The father and son have remained close and are now considering a partnership.

Not all parents are capable later in life of the kind of self-examination and subsequent changes in their behavior that are needed in order to materially improve their relationships with grown sons or daughters who oppose them. But those older parents who are capable of doing so, and who eventually do so, are often rewarded by discovering that their children as adults possess qualities of wisdom and strength which they, the parents, had never before suspected they possessed. Furthermore, parents who can and who finally do get themselves out of the well-worn behavioral ruts of long term parent-child conflict, although advanced in years, often find themselves as a result renewed, with a greater maturity and sense of self-fulfillment than they had ever before realized was possible.

What If You Are Oppositional?

It is sometimes easier to identify oppositional traits in others than to see them in ourselves. But many people do realize that they are to some degree oppositional. What should a person do, one might ask, if he finds himself avoiding the pursuit of cherished goals because of anxieties and unreasonably high levels of perfectionism in himself which are, he feels, the result of parental pressures and criticism?

In overcoming one's own oppositionalism, one should first forgive parents their mistakes, failures, and shortcomings. Oppositional behavior in a child or in an adult is basically a way of punishing parents for their mistakes. An adult who still harbors deep resentment toward his parents is often inclined at crucial moments to defeat himself in the vain attempt to show his parents how wrong they have been. He may be reluctant to succeed for fear that his successes will give pleasure to his parents and confirm their child-rearing practices.

In overcoming oppositionalism, an adult must realize that the role his parents now have is mainly ancient history, and it is absurd, no matter how strong nor how justified he may feel the urge to be, to deprive himself of a productive and meaningful life solely to prove a point. And one should not need nor expect his parents to change. It should be remembered that the childrearing beliefs and practices of parents are the product of what they have been taught; it is unreasonable and unfair to blame them for failing to see the fallacies in these beliefs and the harm of these practices. If one is oppositional, his parents have erred surely, but only in wanting too much for him, and too soon, and if he can understand this fully, he should have little difficulty in forgiving them. Again, it should be said that forgiving one's parents is the first step, and for most, a necessary step, in overcoming oppositionalism in oneself.

Second, one should forgive oneself for mistakes, failures, and shortcomings of the past. And he should forgive himself for those which will surely occur in the future, if and when he pursues the goals he really wants most to pursue. Mistakes are usually retrievable, few failures are fatal, and a person's shortcomings do not necessarily relegate him to a lifetime of ineptitude. One should, of course, hate mistakes with a vengeance, should strive diligently to avoid failures, and should be realistically aware of his own shortcomings. But it has been said, and there is a certain amount of truth to it, that one can never really be considered emotionally mature until he has, at least once in his life, striven with all his ability and energy to achieve a certain cherished goal, and seen himself fail miserably.

The capacity to recover from failure is what is important, not the failure itself. One can avoid mistakes and failures only by never attempting anything, which is the worst mistake and worst failure of all. And one's shortcomings should not be considered shameful. Even the most successful people are poor or only mediocre in most things; they are not judged by their shortcomings, but by the things which they excel at.

The oppositional person must rid himself of the self-defeating habit, ingrained by well-meaning parents and teachers, of concentrating on what he is weak in, and learn to concentrate on developing his intellectual strengths and talents.

Perfectionism and fear of failure are powerful sources of motivation which can propel a person toward greater and greater achievement when he allows himself to take pride in what he has actually done quite well. But these same sources of motivation can paralyze him into rigid inactivity if he forever feels that he must dwell exclusively on the fact, which is always true, that what he has done well could have been done better.

Regardless of how successful a person might be in absolving his parents of blame and in learning to exploit his assets, the third and last injunction he should follow in overcoming oppositionalism is to conscientiously refrain from creating oppositionalism in others. Because he has been pressured and criticized all of his life, the person who is oppositional is highly prone to use these same tactics on others, especially his own children. Strange as it may seem, this is most likely to be the case in the person who has more or less successfully overcome his own oppositionalism.

Oppositional children typically grow up to become pressuring and criticizing parents, giving rise to another generation of oppositional children (and leading some experts in the field to conclude quite erroneously that traits of oppositionalism are inherited).

Learning to refrain from the use of pressure and criticism with one's children and with others, and looking for the best in what others do rather than the worst, has a reciprocal effect. It not only helps prevent others, including one's own children, from acquiring self-defeating oppositional habits, it also helps reduce them.

Once learned, holding back pressure and criticism serves as the most effective method a person can use for annihilating, once and for all, the oppositionalism within himself.

Suggested Readings

Barkley, R.A. Defiant Children. New York: Guilford, 1987.

Brooks, J.B. The Process of Parenting. Palo Alto, California: Mayfield, 1981.

Buntman, P.H., & Saris, E.M. How to Live With Your Teenager. Pasadena, Calif.: Birch Tree Press, 1979.

Clemes, H. & Bean, R. How to Teach Children Responsibility. New York: Price Stern Sloan, 1990

Mac Kenzie, R.J. Setting Limits. Rockland, California: Prima, 1992

Simenon, G. The Disappearance of Odile (trans. Moir, L.). New York: Harcourt Brace Javonovich, 1972

Wachtel, E.F. Treating Troubled Children and Their Families. New York: Guilford, 1994

Williams, R.L., & Long, J.D. Toward a Self-Managed Life Style. Boston: Houghton Mifflin, 1975.